Katherine Stinson

THE FLYING SCHOOLGIRL

Debra L. Winegarten

EAKIN PRESS ◆ Austin, Texas

FIRST EDITION
Copyright © 2000
By Debra L. Winegarten
Published in the United States of America
By Eakin Press
A Division of Sunbelt Media, Inc.
P.O. Drawer 90159 ▱ Austin, Texas 78709-0159
email: eakinpub@sig.net
💻 website: www.eakinpress.com 💻
ALL RIGHTS RESERVED.

1   2   3   4   5   6   7   8   9
1-57168-459-X

Edited by Angela Buckley
Typography by Amber Stanfield

Library of Congress Cataloging-in-Publication Data

Winegarten, Debra L.
    Katherine Stinson : the flying schoolgirl / by Debra L. Winegarten.
        p.   cm.
    Includes bibliographical references.
    ISBN 1-57168-459-X (hardcover)
    1. Stinson, Katherine 1891-1977--Juvenile literature. 2. Women air pilots--United
States--Biography--Juvenile literature. 3. Women architects--United States--Biography--
Juvenile literature. [1. Stinson, Katherine 1891-1977. 2. Air pilots. 3. Women--
Biography.] I.Title
TL540.S827 W55 2000
629.13'092--dc21   00-059285

This book is dedicated to
my heart partner, C. Huyser,
who loves to fly with me.

Contents

Acknowledgments

My thanks to my mother, Ruthe Winegarten, for first introducing me to Katherine Stinson. Special thanks to the librarians and staff of the Women's Collection at Texas Woman's University for their encouragement and for keeping the archives with Katherine's story safe and available to the public: Elizabeth Snapp, Dawn Letson, Nancy Marshall Durr, and Ann Barton.

Thanks to my father, Al Winegarten, for explaining to me the nuances of airplane flying and instrumentation, for taking me for my first flight (that I remember) in a helicopter, and for sharing his love of flying with me. Thanks to my brother, Marc Sanders, for his continual encouragement as this book progressed, and to my sister, Martha Wilson, for always reminding me not to take myself too seriously.

Many thanks to Sharon Kahn for her thoughtful reading of and suggestions for the manuscript. Thanks to ASB for always believing in my abilities and urging me on. Special thanks to Cindy for all the essential background support and motivation on a daily basis.

Thanks to Tim O'Krongley, manager of Stinson Field in San Antonio, for letting me pick his brain and his photograph collection to aid this book's visuals, as well as for helping with the factual information and anecdotes. Thanks to Elizabeth Pillsworth and Ann Massmann at the

University of New Mexico, Albuquerque, for their excellent help in obtaining gorgeous photos from the Stinson-Otero Collection.

Finally, my heartfelt thanks to Ed Eakin and his staff for helping turn this dream into a reality.

This book was prepared using a variety of reference materials, including primary and secondary sources. I have tried to stay as faithful and as close to the original texts as possible. I have taken liberties with the conversations between Katherine and her family because there are no existing records of these. I invented her friend, Elizabeth, to accompany Katherine on some of her journeys. Any mistakes as a result of using these literary devices are entirely my own. The original materials are available in the Women's Collection at Texas Woman's University Library in Denton, Texas.

Chapter 1

The Dream That Wouldn't Go Away

"Mother, we've got to talk right now," yelled Katherine after racing home from her piano lesson. She threw her music on the kitchen table, and the cake her mother had been baking all afternoon fell in the oven. Emma Stinson sighed. It was August 12, 1910, summer was in full swing, and the day was steaming hot. They were to celebrate Mr. Stinson's birthday that night.

Emma knew from the excited tone of Katherine's voice that something big was brewing. Her daughter rarely showed quite this much excitement. Emma poured two glasses of iced tea with lemon and pulled her daughter into the drawing room of their small home in Jackson, Mississippi. She handed Katherine a cool glass streaming with droplets and leaned back in her chair to hear her daughter's latest story.

"My piano teacher, Miss Magruder, says that by the end of the summer she will have taught me everything she knows. She thinks I should go to Europe to continue my musical studies.

Mother, you know how much I want to be a music teacher. We've just got to figure out a way for me to study abroad." Katherine, nineteen, had been playing the piano since she was nine.

Emma Stinson sighed deeply for the second time that sultry afternoon. She didn't believe in discouraging the dreams of her children. How could she tell Katherine that the family budget would never stretch far enough for such an undertaking? She struggled to find a way to gently break this news to her daughter. As if she sensed what her mother was going to say, Katherine interrupted another sigh.

"I've thought about all the different things I could do to earn money for the trip," offered Katherine. "I could type, teach music, or clerk in a department store. The problem with all of those options is that I'll be ninety years old before I can save enough money to study in Europe. Mother, you've just got to help me find another way!"

Katherine's parents were divorced in 1904, and Emma was raising the four Stinson children herself. Emma knew all too well how hard money was to come by. Still, she saw from the determined look in Katherine's eyes that her daughter was not giving up this dream.

"Katherine, you know I believe in you and your ability to reach your goals. I must say, however, this time you've gone too far. I haven't the slightest idea where we can find the money for you to study music in Europe," said Emma.

Unsettled by her mother's reply, Katherine let her eyes fall to the coffee table, where the *Jackson Daily Herald* was lying. A headline shouted, "Barnstormers Bring Home $1,000 a Day." Snatching the paper from the table, Katherine waved it under her mother's nose. "This is it!" she shouted, jumping up from her chair. "This is how I can earn the money. I'll learn to fly an airplane!"

Overtaken by Katherine's enthusiasm, Emma Stinson could almost see the gears turning in her daughter's head. Little did she suspect that in a few years her oldest child would literally turn head over "wheels" as she looped-the-loop thousands of feet in the air.

At the same instant, both mother and daughter had the same thought. How on earth could they get Papa Stinson to agree? He already considered Katherine unmanageable and wanted her to settle down and lead a normal life—to get married and have some grandchildren for him to bounce on his knees.

But Katherine was eager to share her latest dream with her father. She decided to tell him the truth. That evening, after his birthday party, Katherine cornered the visiting Papa Stinson. She was sure he'd be in a receptive mood after enjoying an evening of good food, laughter, and celebration, surrounded by his children.

"Papa," began Katherine, with a twinkle in her eye.

"Now, Katie," her father interrupted, "I hope you're going to give me the birthday present I've been waiting for, by telling me you've finally decided on a beau and are going to settle down and get married."

"Actually, Papa," Katherine said, sparkling with enthusiasm, "that's exactly what I want to talk to you about."

Papa Stinson sat bolt upright in his chair, barely able to believe his ears. Somehow Katherine always managed to avoid talking to him seriously about getting married. For the first time he could remember, Katherine was agreeing to discuss marriage. He was thrilled!

"Now, Papa," Katherine began again, "I do indeed hope to fall in love someday, marry, and raise a family. However, I must be honest with you. Right now there's no one I'm thinking about spending the rest of my life with. There's no one I'm even remotely fond of! I also don't want to have to rely on you and Mama forever to support me. That's why I'm studying hard to be a music teacher, so that I can take care of myself."

"But Katie," Papa Stinson protested.

"Don't interrupt me now, Papa, I need to have my say here. Papa, I've thought long and hard about this. To advance in my musical studies, I have to travel to Europe to work with the best teachers and musicians. I know that you and Mama can't afford to pay my way to Europe or support me while I'm over there."

"But Katie," her father broke in again.

"Papa, please let me finish," Katherine begged her father. "I've got it all figured out. I'm going to learn to fly an airplane, because barnstormers can earn up to a thousand dollars a day or more. At that rate, I can earn twenty thousand dollars in just a month, which would be more than enough money to pay for flying lessons, buy a plane, and study in Europe," she ended with a flourish. "And who knows?" she asked, her eyes shining brightly. "I might even find a handsome beau during all that traveling and get married, to boot!"

Katherine's keen powers of persuasion soon brought her reluctant father around to her way of thinking. Katherine presented flying as a means to an end. Teaching music was, after all, a very respectable profession for a young woman.

Chapter 2
Riding in a Hot Air Balloon

Katherine's first flying experience came the following year—not in an airplane, but in a hot air balloon. While visiting friends in Kansas City, Missouri, she heard about a balloonist, Lieutenant H. B. Honeywell, who was carrying passengers aloft. Out of 250 people who applied for the trip, Katherine was one of four chosen for the unique adventure. On August 31, 1911, Katherine made her first trip skyward.

Katherine could hardly wait to go home to Mississippi to tell her family about her balloon experience. Gathering them all together after dinner in their drawing room, she excitedly described the ascension of the hot air ballon to her mother and her siblings, Eddie, Marjorie, and Jack.

"I was amazed at the freedom I felt while in the air," she explained. "Gazing down at the earth, I felt like a bird as I watched the wheat fields and farmhouses pass below me. I wasn't frightened by the altitude or the gentle swaying of the balloon basket as we sailed in the breeze. I am now more determined than ever to learn to fly!" It was clear that Katherine was not discouraged. The flight in the hot air balloon had instead deepened her determination to become an aviatrix. Mrs. Stinson smiled at her daughter's courage.

Katherine's next step was to find someone to give her flying lessons. Not only would she have to convince someone to teach a five-foot-tall, 101-pound young woman to fly; she would also have to raise $500 to pay for the lessons. Once again, a lack of money threatened to put an end to Katherine's ambition.

Bracing herself, Katherine turned to her mother for support. "Mother," she stated firmly, "I need to talk to you right now." Mrs. Stinson knew that this phrase always preceded an outrageous request from her older daughter, so she settled back in her chair cushions to listen.

"You know the piano that I won in the city competition?" Katherine asked her mother rhetorically. "We have to sell it so that I can pay for my flying lessons."

"Sell it?" Mrs. Stinson was shocked. "Katherine, that would be like throwing the fishing rod into the river to catch a fish! How on earth will you be able to give piano lessons if we sell the piano?" her mother wanted to know.

"Once I learn to fly, I can make enough money in a week to buy twenty pianos. But if I don't learn to fly, I'll never study music in Europe, so the piano won't do me any good anyway," Katherine answered tearfully. This argument left Mrs. Stinson speechless, as she could find no flaw in her daughter's logic.

Word went out the next day that the Stinson piano was for sale. Within a week, Katherine was $200 richer and one piano poorer. She missed the piano a lot, and she still needed $300 more. Katherine paid her father a visit.

"Papa," she said, "I want to make you proud of me."

"I am proud of you, honey," Papa Stinson replied.

"Hear me out," Katherine insisted. "I need three hundred dollars more so that I can take flying lessons and make my dream of European music lessons come true. Will you lend me the money?" she asked.

At first Papa Stinson thought he'd end these silly plans once and for all. He came close to refusing, but the look in his daughter's eyes stopped him. He could see the tears welling just below the surface, and he knew how much courage it had taken for Katherine to ask him for the money. He agreed to lend it to her, but she would have to pay it back in two years.

With the loan from her father in hand, Katherine set out for St. Louis, Missouri, in search of a flying instructor.

Katherine Stinson with her flight instructor, Max Lillie.

Chapter 3

Learning to Fly

In January 1912 Katherine arrived at Kinloch Field near St. Louis, Missouri, where she planned to take flying lessons at Tom Benoist's flying school. The first person to take Katherine on an actual airplane flight was to be Tony Jannus, one of the greatest aviators at that time.

"What's a little imp like you want to do with flying?" Jannus asked Katherine.

"I've been up in a hot air balloon," Katherine explained, "and it was the most thrilling experience I've ever had. I want to learn flying for a lot of different reasons. I love the excitement of being so high in the air, soaring with the birds, moving so fast, and seeing all the sights below me. Besides, exhibition pilots make good money, and it's a chance for me to finance my musical career."

Jannus thought Katherine much too small to be trusted with the controls of such a big machine. Instead of giving her a real flying lesson, he decided to teach her a little lesson of his own. It was freezing in St. Louis on the afternoon of January 21. Snow covered the ground. The air was bitterly cold, and Katherine could see her breath when she exhaled. She climbed into the Benoist Model 12 airplane and took the passenger's seat behind Jannus. Once strapped in, Jannus took off into the air, climbed the plane to about a thousand feet, banked steeply, and began orbiting the field.

Katherine later described the flight:

> I had expected to sail along on an even keel, and this standing on edge in the air struck me as a queer performance. It occurred to me then to wonder how much he knew about flying, anyway, and I finally decided to ask him to straighten out the machine, simply to find out whether he could do it. I shouted at him several times and he paid absolutely no attention to me. I didn't like that; so I kept on shouting, until I suddenly realized that I couldn't hear even the sound of my own voice because of the noise of the engine.
>
> Then I pulled at his sleeve, and when he looked around, I motioned him to straighten it out. I remember how he laughed. I know he thought I was frightened. But I wasn't. I just wanted to find out whether he could do it. When I found that he could, I was perfectly satisfied. We stayed up twenty minutes—it seemed to me only about five. And instead of being cured of my ambition, as I think Mr. Jannus hoped, I came down more eager than ever to become a flyer myself.

Little had Jannus known that Katherine was not the fearful type. She pressured him to give her lessons the following week, and he agreed, although reluctantly. Tom Benoist, the owner of the flying field, was still uncertain of Katherine's abilities. Privately, he told Jannus, "If she doesn't crash, she's sure to catch pneumonia up there." Jannus didn't want any part in discouraging Katherine's flying dreams. He had already bumped heads with her and come up a little bruised. Jannus also believed that Katherine could be a good pilot, for in her lessons she had demonstrated a natural aptitude for flying.

Despite Katherine's insistence on continuing her training flights, Benoist convinced Jannus to join him in sending her packing. They told her to go home and advised her to pursue a more lady-like profession.

"Katherine," they told her, "you're just too pretty and petite. At a hundred pounds, you have no business being trusted with the controls of such a manly device as an airplane. There's just too much power there, and the winds are too strong and unpredictable. There's no way you'll be able to control the aircraft if something should go wrong. You'd do a lot better to find a job more suited for a woman your size, like teaching." Apparently, the ideas of the time as to the proper place for a woman clouded the two men's ability to see Katherine's great potential as a pilot.

Talk of this kind made Katherine mad. She was used to her mother's philosophy. Emma Stinson said she "saw no reason why members of the 'gentler' sex should not do pretty much as they pleased—even to the point of entering what were considered to be strictly 'men's' occupations." Seeing that the two men had made up their minds and weren't going to teach her, Katherine packed her bags and headed for Chicago.

In Chicago the winds of good fortune began to blow Katherine's way. While visiting Cicero Field in late May of 1912, Katherine, now twenty-one, met Maximillian Theodore Liljestrand, who was from Sweden. He had just organized a flying school. Enchanted by Katherine's passion for flying, Maximillian told her, "Just call me Max Lillie," and enrolled her in his school.

Unlike the previous flight instructors, Max was not concerned about Katherine's size and sex. He saw Katherine's quick grasp for the mechanics of the airplane's operation, as well as her inborn dexterity, so necessary for flying. Her ability to think clearly and act quickly further convinced Max that she had what it took to become an excellent pilot.

Katherine concentrated just as hard on her flying lessons as she had on her piano lessons. For two weeks, she trained in a Wright "B" airplane, learning to read the instruments and getting a feel for the controls. After in-the-air instruction totaling only four hours and ten minutes, Katherine was ready to fly solo. Of the three women pilots licensed to fly in the United States, two had died in fatal crashes the month before Katherine first flew alone.

The day that Katherine was scheduled to fly solo, Max, somewhat nervous, asked her, "Are you sure you want to fly today, Katie?" A quick nod of her head assured him that she was ready. Max cranked the propeller, and Katherine lifted the plane smoothly into the air. She performed two required figure-eights and was about to start the altitude test, when suddenly her motor stopped. Her heart stopped, too.

"Come down here, Katie!" Max shouted. "Quickly!" Katherine pulled the Wright "B" plane around for an emergency landing and reached the ground safely. Three days later, on July 16, 1912, she completed the 500-foot altitude test. At the age of twenty-one, Katherine Stinson became the fourth female pilot in the United States to qualify for the *Fédération Aéronautique*

*Katherine Stinson was the fourth woman in the U.S. to qualify
for her pilot's license.*

Internationale, or FAI, pilot's certificate. The FAI issued her license number 148, dated July 24, 1912. Although her pilot's license lists her birth year as 1893, Katherine was actually born in 1891. Because she had such a youthful apperance, questions about her age followed her throughout her flying career.

Katherine spent the rest of the summer of 1912 flying practice lessons at Cicero Field. She returned to the family farm in Hot Springs, Arkansas, for the winter. Katherine paid a visit to her father to update him on her recent trip to the Midwest.

"So, Katie," Papa Stinson asked his daughter, "when are you going to get on with this flying business so you can earn enough money for your music lessons in Europe?" Secretly proud of her achievements, Mr. Stinson kept his pride hidden behind a gruff exterior.

"Soon, Papa, soon," she assured him. "First," she continued, "I have to buy an airplane, and then, before you know it, I will have earned enough money to pay for my trip to Europe and back again!" But her love for flying had replaced her love for music. Deep in her heart, Katherine knew that she would never return to the piano.

Katherine Stinson's Aviation Milestones, 1911–1915

August 31, 1911
Katherine takes her first ride aloft, in a hot air balloon in Kansas City, Missouri.

January 21, 1912
Has her first plane ride at Kinloch Field in St. Louis, Missouri.

May 1912
Begins flying lessons with Max Lillie at Cicero Field in Chicago, Illinois.

July 24, 1912
Is issued license number 148 by the *Fédération Aéronautique Internationale,* becoming the fourth woman in the U.S. to receive her pilot's license.

April 1913
Founds and becomes president of the Stinson Aviation Company with Abner Cook as vice president and her mother, Emma Beavers Stinson, as secretary/treasurer.

September 24, 1913
Becomes the first pilot in the U.S. to carry pioneer airmail during the Montana State Fair.

December 1913
Becomes the first woman to fly over London, England.

June 1914
Becomes the first woman to fly alone at night.

July 18, 1915
Becomes the first women in the world to loop-the-loop, at Grant Park in Chicago, Illinois.

November 21, 1915
First performs the "dippy twist" loop, a stunt she invented.

December 17, 1915
Becomes the first pilot to perform skywriting, spelling out C-A-L over the night sky in Los Angeles.

Chapter 4

Plane Shopping

True to her word, Katherine began searching for ways to buy an airplane. Once again, she was faced with the dilemma of finding money.

"Mother, can we talk?" The familiar phrase hit Emma Stinson's ears. Katherine told her mother that everyone she had met in the aviation industry had enormous enthusiasm for flying. Being a visionary, Katherine saw a tremendous opportunity to make airplanes and sell them to others. Only a few businesses were actually making planes.

Eddie, one of Katherine's two younger brothers, had also caught airplane fever. He had traveled to Chicago to study airplane mechanics

Katherine Stinson at the controls with her younger brother Jack.

and flying. Marjorie, Katherine's younger sister, had caught the flying bug as well. The entire Stinson family was swept up into Katherine's aviation dreams, including Emma Stinson.

Emma had a great deal of confidence in Katherine's ability to make her dreams become reality. Katherine had a great deal of confidence in her mother's business sense. Together, in April 1913, the two of them incorporated as the Stinson Aviation Company, to "manufacture, sell, rent and otherwise engage in the aircraft trade." The new company's first source of income would be the flying fees earned by Katherine during her exhibitions and barnstorming events.

Therefore, Stinson Aviation's first order of business was to buy a plane for Katherine to fly so that she could earn money for the fledgling company. After borrowing $3,070 from friends and relatives, Katherine returned to Chicago to buy her first plane from her old friend and teacher, Max Lillie. Max had modified a Wright "B" airplane, and he sold it to Katherine for $2,000.

The next day, an incident occurred at Cicero Airfield that initially gave the male pilots quite a laugh. Anxious to examine the condition of her new plane, Katherine appeared early in the morning with a bucket of soapy water and a huge scrub brush.

"Hey, Katie," one man called. "What's the matter? Afraid you'll get your hands dirty flying your new plane?" The men gathered around Katherine's airplane to see what their female counterpart was doing.

"Isn't that just like a woman?" another asked as he watched Katherine scrubbing furiously away at the dirt and grime that had accumulated on the wires of the plane's wings during the months it had sat idly on the ground. The men's jokes only made her more determined to clean up her machine.

Katherine wrote later:

> Judging from my own experience, I think women would be more careful in this respect than men are. I remember, for instance, how the men laughed at me when I bought my first machine. It was one of the old type, which I got from Mr. Lillie, and I immediately set to work to have it cleaned up. The wings were covered with dirt, the wires and joints were gummed with oil. I went over every inch of it; scrubbed the plane, polished the wires, and cleaned the joints. The men thought I was a regular old maid about it. They said I would ruin the cloth with my scrubbing, and that the oil didn't hurt the wires and joints, anyway.
>
> I was young, very conscious of my inexperience, and secretly I wondered if they were right and if my scrubbing would injure the plane. But I wanted to see the condition of things under all that dirt. And I really did find that a good many wires needed to be replaced!

While the men made fun of her and called her a spinster, Katherine found dangerous wires and fittings encrusted with grease that obviously needed replacing. Hidden beneath all the dirt, these broken parts could spell instant death for a pilot in the air.

With a new sense of respect for the female pilot, the men scurried back to their own planes and began examining them a little more closely than usual. Katherine had begun a tradition that she would follow throughout her flying career—the thorough and careful inspection and maintenance of her plane before each flight.

As she told her friend Max Lillie over dinner that night, "It's all right if your car goes wrong while you're driving it. You can get out in the road and tinker with it. But if your airplane breaks down, you can't sit on a convenient cloud and tinker with *that*! So, it behooves you to try and make sure that it won't break down." Little did she realize the prophetic nature of her words to Max.

A week later, Katherine's plane gleamed, and she was satisfied that all the movable parts were in good working condition. As she prepared for her first series of barnstorming events, a reporter approached her and asked, "Aren't you afraid to fly?"

"If I were afraid to fly, I certainly shouldn't do it," she blurted out. "The only thing I fear about flying is catching cold. Sneezing is the real cause of many fatal crashes." The reporter couldn't decide if she was joking or not.

Katherine Stinson performing a preflight inspection of her plane. She was careful to check every wire and mechanism before each flight.

Chapter 5

Mountain Flying in Montana

Throughout her flying career, people insisted on asking Katherine questions about her fear. Because flying was such an innovation in those times, Katherine often thought that reporters were simply "airing" their own fears related to flying, not hers.

"My mother never warned me not to do this or that for fear of being hurt," Katherine told reporters from Ohio to Indiana. "Of course, I got hurt, but I was never afraid. If I think my machine is all right and I know I can manage it, I am not afraid."

"Miss Stinson, aren't you afraid your machine will fall?" asked a curious reporter on Labor Day, 1913, in Pine Bluff, Arkansas.

"My goodness, if I were afraid, I certainly wouldn't be in this business!" she retorted.

Flying did pose some physical challenges, however. When seated in her aircraft, Katherine

Katherine trained for only four hours and ten minutes before taking and passing her pilot's exam.

perched precariously on a narrow rigging fitted to the leading edge of the lower wing. She often joked that the engine provided her heating system at high altitudes, while the lack of a windshield gave her natural air conditioning. In this early machine, very little protected her from the elements, and she was often brutally buffeted by the wind.

Bill Pickens, who had begun managing her professional affairs, would later recall, "There she was, a little wisp of a thing with big brown eyes, an engagingly soft southern drawl and pink ribbons in her long curls. She didn't look a day over sixteen." Because of her youthful appearance, Pickens booked Katherine as "The School Girl Who Outflies the Men." This title was later shortened to "The Flying Schoolgirl," a name that stuck with her throughout her entire flying career. Newspapers dubbed her "The Queen of the Skies."

Katherine, "The Flying Schoolgirl," had become the nation's most famous aerial attraction. Katherine thrilled large crowds with her graceful flying and firm control, executing a number of exciting patterns that almost always ended in a smooth, perfect landing. A. J. Breitenstein, the secretary of the 1913 Montana State Fair Association, concocted the idea of having Katherine be a pilot at the state fair's air meet in Helena, Montana, September 22–27. Katherine arrived there with her $5,000 Wright biplane on September 16 to begin preparations for her first flight in the mountains.

Katherine's plane, exhibited on the midway in the aerodrome, gave many local residents their first-ever glimpse of an airplane. The Wright "B" was a primitive open aircraft made of spruce and wire with muslin-covered wings.

The Wright brothers, Wilbur and Orville, had made their first successful flight just ten years before, in 1903. News traveled a lot more slowly then than it does now, either through word-of-mouth, letters, telegrams, or the newspapers. Although radio had been invented, at the time the technology was mainly used as a means for ships to communicate. Most people in rural America didn't have access to telephones. Because of this limited communication, very few people knew much about airplanes.

The local press besieged Katherine with questions about her new-fangled machine. Patiently, Katherine answered, "No, I do not intend to take any passengers aloft. Yes, I have been worried about mountain flying, not because of the height of the mountains, but because of the lack of flat landing spaces, which is so crucial to airplane safety. If my engine should stall, I need a safe place to set down, and get it started up again. I must say that after scouting the area, I'm glad I don't have to take off from the side of a hill!"

By this time, Katherine knew that flying was going to be the focus of her life, and she took her work seriously. She was constantly on the lookout for new flying venues, as well as new stunts. She decided she wanted to carry mail as part of her Helena appearance. Ever the charmer, she told George Landstrun, Helena's postmaster, of her desire to be an airmail pilot. Landstrun immediately wired Postmaster General Albert Sidney Burleson in Washington, D.C., and got quick approval for the plan. Katherine's airmail postal route was designated number 663,002. Next, Landstrun erected an aerial postal substation on the Helena fairgrounds.

In an official ceremony, Katherine took an oath to "support the Constitution and to defend the

mails." This ceremony made Katherine a bona fide government employee, duly sworn in and officially proclaimed. Now she would become America's first woman to carry the United States airmail.

The Montana State Fair opened on September 22, 1913, but Katherine found herself grounded. Dangerous winds went whistling through the Helena Valley and the surrounding peaks. Katherine decided the conditions were much too dangerous to make her mail run. Disappointed, she postponed her first airmail flight.

The next day, the weather was perfect for flying. Gathering her mail, which consisted mostly of postcards bearing her own likeness, Katherine took off, soaring across the high valley and almost disappearing past the pine trees over the horizon. She dropped her mail pouch near a substation, where postal employee C. B. Anderson canceled the mail, then sent it on its way through normal postal channels.

Katherine delivered an astonishing total of 1,333 pieces during those four days at the fair. She also flew the mail on two later occasions, once in Troy, Alabama, on November 3–8, 1914, and again in Tucson, Arizona, November 4–6, 1915. Not only was Katherine the first woman to fly pioneer airmail, she is the only woman to have carried it three times.

Her first summer barnstorming in 1913 was a smashing success. Crowds gathered in cornfields and cotton fields throughout the South and Midwest to watch the dainty "schoolgirl" per-

Katherine Stinson receiving a bag of airmail for delivery in Tucson, Arizona, in November 1915. She was the first woman authorized to carry the U.S. airmail.

form. At the age of twenty-two, Katherine was hardly a schoolgirl. Reporters kept trying to figure out how old she actually was. Katherine kept her age a secret, as that added to her mystique.

Thrilled by the public's response to her flying, Katherine made her way to San Antonio, Texas, where her friend Max Lillie had relocated. Winters were mild in that historic city, home of the Alamo. Max had determined that South Texas winters were far preferable to the windy, snowy conditions of Chicago's Cicero Field. He gained permission to use space at Fort Sam Houston to house his planes and run a flight school. Katherine soon convinced her whole family to join her in moving to San Antonio.

As San Antonians began to get used to the sight of Katherine flying overhead in her Wright "B" plane, tragedy struck. Her good friend and teacher, Max Lillie, plunged to his death when his plane broke apart in midair. While Katherine had been so scrupulous about maintenance, Max had simply ignored it. This lack of concern cost him his life.

Although Max's death affected her greatly, Katherine refused to give up flying. "Back to the question of fear: I am not afraid to fly," she told another set of reporters. "I know that if nothing happens to the machine I am safe. And I try to make sure of my machine. Confidence is back of it all. And it seems to me so simple to say, 'Well, if other people have done this I don't see why I can't.' I think I should feel like saying that about anything I wanted very much to do."

When it came to flying, there was very little that Katherine believed she could not do.

Katherine Stinson's Aviation Milestones, 1916–1918

January 18, 1916
Katherine, Eddie, and Marjorie sign a lease with the City of San Antonio to develop land where they eventually establish the Stinson School of Flying. The land is now known as Stinson Field.

December 1916
Becomes the first woman pilot to fly in Japan and China.

June 24, 1917
Raises over $2 million in pledges for the Red Cross.

December 11, 1917
Sets a new national record for both nonstop distance and endurance, flying 610 miles in nine hours and ten minutes, from San Diego to San Francisco.

June 1, 1918
Sets a new duration record of ten hours and ten minutes by flying airmail from Chicago to New York. The trip is 783 miles by railroad standards and inaugurates this airmail route.

July 9, 1918
Carries the first airmail for the Canadian government.

September 26, 1918
Becomes the first female airmail pilot for the U.S. Post Office Department.

Chapter 6

Marjorie Joins the Action

As Katherine began spending more and more time in the air, her confidence in her ability as a pilot soared as well. She spent much of 1914 perfecting her flying skills at country fairs across the U.S. In June 1914 she became the first woman to fly alone at night.

Katherine had done so well with exhibition flying that Marjorie, her younger sister, decided it was time to join in the action. Marjorie pestered Katherine endlessly to give her lessons. Katherine always refused, but Marjorie was every bit as determined to learn to fly as her older sister had been.

Legend has it that Katherine taught Marjorie to fly in two hours while on the ground, using only a mop in an old wash bucket to show Marjorie how to control the rudder. However, this is just a fanciful tale. The truth can be learned by taking a little peek into Marjorie's diary:

The Stinson sisters,
Marjorie and Katherine, sharing a joke.

June 25 (1914):

On the train for Dayton—object—to learn to fly at the Wright School. Estimated time required—six weeks. I have not risked writing for information about flight training for fear that girls might be discouraged in this so-called hazardous undertaking. I expect to just breeze in, introduce myself, offer them the check for tuition, then try to talk them into taking me.

Since I have already had six flights with my sister Katherine I feel almost used to the air, but so far I have been very much occupied with the business of holding on to the struts for dear life, and have been unable to persuade Katie to give me any lessons because, as she put it, she was afraid I might hurt myself and so preferred not to teach me.

Unfortunately, things didn't go quite as smoothly as Marjorie had envisioned.

Noon—arrived safely in Dayton, established myself at the Algonquin Hotel, called at Wright Factory in town. Gosh! In spite of my longest skirt, they had the nerve to ask whether I was eighteen yet and I had to admit I wasn't, and in consequence of my infancy had to wire home for permission to learn to fly. Meantime, Mr. Orville Wright took me out to his flying field where I saw the original hangar, the old launching device used before wheels were put on planes, the school plane and the man who is to teach me to fly, Mr. Howard Rinehart. The permission was waiting when I returned to the hotel.

Wind and rain constantly hampered Marjorie's attempts to learn to fly, as the school did not give lessons during bad weather. No lessons were given on Sundays, either. In addition, every time a new pilot showed up, he was given preference over Marjorie, so that she was constantly fighting, cajoling, and doing everything in her power to make sure she got her flying time in. Actual time spent in the air ranged from two to twenty minutes per flight, with a lot of the instruction done on the ground using a variety of balancing machines to help give the new aviators the feel for flying in the air. Often, the flight lesson consisted only of taking off and then landing.

Although it was hard to get her flight time in, Marjorie persevered. In her diary, she wrote of the days before she tested for her pilot's license.

August 4, 1914

A.M. Something broken. No flying.

P.M. Fixed again, one flight with Rinehart and one 2 minute flight alone, also one set of figures eight alone. It was great to look over and not see Rinehart beside me. I knew exactly who was flying then, and I could almost hear the other students' sigh of relief when I stepped out of the plane leaving it all in one piece, that they might later fly in it. Finding myself alone and able to go around the much beaten path of eights, I even wished I could go faster than the alleged 40 miles per hour.

August 5, 1914

A.M. Last night I dreamed I was flying eights and making thousands of high altitude landings. May the practice be of benefit today!

P.M. Made other set of eights and altitude flight and then walked away from the plane leaving it intact for the remaining students. Six weeks to the day [from the start of lessons]. At last, I have my pilot's license, after flying instruction totaling 4½ hours!

After only four and a half hours of flying instructions from Howard Rinehart, Marjorie had flown her solo flight and passed her flying certification test. That may not seem like a long time, but it had taken her six weeks to complete those four-plus hours of air time. Marjorie earned her pilot's license at the age of seventeen, becoming the youngest female pilot in the U.S. and the ninth woman ever to receive a pilot's license. She received license number 303 from the FAI, issued on August 12, 1914.

"I knew I was going to be a flyer by the time I was twelve," Marjorie said. "I hung around the airport working for my lessons. The mechanics let me help them, probably because my hands were smaller than anyone else's so I could reach places they couldn't. When other girls were playing with dolls, I was building airplane models. I think any female can make it in anything she really wants to if she can get the proper training and education."

Marjorie had worked hard to get the proper training to become a pilot. She later became the first pilot inducted into the U.S. Aviation Corps at the age of nineteen, adding to her accomplishment as the youngest licensed pilot in the country. She would soon join her older sister in a venture that would shape the future of flying in the United States.

By 1915 Katherine was searching for new ways to showcase her flying abilities. Male pilots were beginning to perform daring stunts in their planes, and Katherine was eager to join in the fun. When trying stunts for the first time, she told herself, "Other people have done it! And if they can do it, I don't see why I can't."

With this attitude, she learned the feat called the "loop-the-loop." Because the few male pilots

Marjorie and Katherine Stinson in a modified Wright "B" plane, named after its inventors, Orville and Wilbur Wright, who originally made bicycles. Bicycle tires were used on these early planes.

who had mastered the loop-the-loop thought it was too dangerous for Katherine to perform, they refused to teach her how to do it. Undaunted, Katherine taught herself and became the fourth pilot and the first woman to complete the stunt. In July 1915 a Chicago crowd watched as she became the first woman in the world to loop-the-loop. In a six-month period, Katherine looped-the-loop over 500 times without an accident.

What made the loop-the-loop so potentially dangerous was the frequent tendency of a small airplane's engine to stall when reaching the highest point in the loop. When this happened, the plane fell toward the ground, and the pilot was doomed unless she had the ability to restart her engine. A key factor in restarting the engine was the pilot going high enough in the first place to give her time to crank the motor up again, should the engine fail. Katherine's experience and knowledge led her to add extra altitude to her loops, just in case she found herself in that situation. Some pilots failed to restart their engines, and crowds often feared a crash during a pilot's loop-the-loop stunt. But when Katherine described what the stunt felt like, fear wasn't on her mind:

> In looping-the-loop you do not seem to leave straight flying. The earth seems to go around you. First, the earth rises until it is perpendicular, the houses and trees sticking out from it as from a wall. Next the earth moves until the houses and trees appear to hang over you. Then the earth looks like an upright wall on the other side until finally everything takes its normal place beneath you. All the while, you seem to be flying straight. A most curious sensation.
>
> And when you fly upside down you don't feel as if you had turned over. Rather, you feel as if the earth had changed places with the sky and was hanging over you.

Merely looping-the-loop wasn't good enough for Katherine. She expanded on this feat by developing her "dippy twist" loop, a vertical bank in which the aircraft rolled wing over wing when the top of the loop was reached. She first performed the dippy twist maneuver on November 21, 1915. On her next flight, she made eight consecutive loops, flew upside down for thirty seconds, and executed a series of spiral spins.

Constantly compared to male pilots, Katherine worked hard to equal or outdo their stunts. The dippy twist loop was actually a clever combination of two separate stunts—a loop-the-loop and a snap roll. She later told reporters, "When I looped-the-loop last July, it was a bitter pill for the male pilots to swallow, but I accomplished all their stunts and in my case went them one better." Katherine was undoubtedly the first woman precision flier, and she is often given credit for being the first precision flier of either sex.

Throughout her flying career, she continued to perfect crowd-pleasing stunts. Men often criticized her stunt work. They claimed that audiences would assume that if a woman could do them, the stunts must be easy. This notion, they said, would "cause foolhardy men to try them and might lead to their deaths." Katherine, however, stood her ground, firmly believing her stunts would be an integral part of aviation.

Katherine's daring spirit caused newspaper reporters to follow her everywhere. When later asked about her musical education and her plans for pursuing her musical career, Katherine was brief. "Somehow, I never got around to it. The only music I'm interested in now is the music of my motor and the hum of the wind in the struts of my Wright airplane." Reporters constantly recorded her adventures, and Katherine's name soon became a household word throughout the United States.

Chapter 7

Night Skywriting

"Katherine, can we talk?" Emma Stinson asked during one of her daughter's rare visits home in 1915. Katherine usually started these conversations, but this time it was her turn to listen.

"With all the traveling you're doing these days," her mother said, "it doesn't look proper for a single woman to be flying all across the country alone."

Katherine Stinson enjoyed racing cars almost as much as she loved flying planes.

"Mother, you're simply being old-fashioned," Katherine objected.

"Let me finish. I know you don't have time to catch a husband with all the hours you spend in the air, but you need someone to protect you when you're on the ground. I don't worry about you when you're sailing through the clouds; I know you can take care of yourself up there. When you land in new cities with strange men around is when I start to worry. What if one of them tries to carry you off?" her mother wondered aloud.

"No one would dream of such a thing!" Katherine answered. Secretly, though, she knew that her mother had a good point. She often carried with her the large sums of money that she earned at flying exhibitions. And the most dangerous weapon she carried was a pair of knitting needles. Due to her small size, she would be in big trouble if someone tried to hurt her.

"What do you suggest?" Katherine asked her mother. "Surely you're not thinking of going with me?" The thought of her mother holding on for dear life as Katherine flew upside down nearly made her laugh out loud.

"Well, Katherine, I've been thinking long and hard about this, and I have an idea. What you need is someone who could drive a car from one town to the next. That person could deliver your luggage and make overnight arrangements for you, as well as meet you when you land," her mother suggested.

The idea sounded good to Katherine. She was tired of landing in cities where she knew no one. She hated not having someone to tell her daily adventures to (besides reporters). She dreaded spending evenings alone in unfamiliar places. The thought of having a friendly face meet her was appealing.

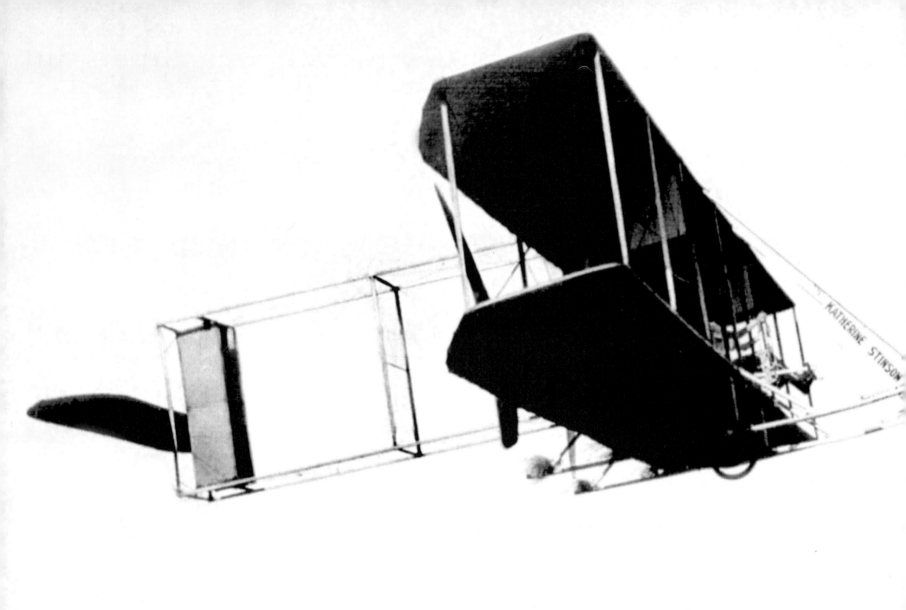

Sensing that her daughter was about to agree with her, Mrs. Stinson continued, "I even know the perfect person! Remember your old friend Elizabeth? Her husband died two months ago, and the poor girl hasn't been herself. She has no job, no children, just doesn't seem to know what to do with her time. Don't you see that if she went with you, why, it would help the both of you? What do you think?"

The idea delighted Katherine. She told her mother, "What a fine idea! I shall drive over to Elizabeth's right now and offer her the job. I wonder why I didn't think of this before?" Katherine raced out the door and headed for Elizabeth's house.

Mrs. Stinson settled back in her chair, a contented smile crossing her face. She knew that Katherine's enthusiasm would win Elizabeth over in an instant.

Two weeks later, Katherine and Elizabeth set out for California, Katherine in her airplane and Elizabeth in a car filled with suitcases and dreams for the future.

In California, Katherine again dazzled the crowds with her breathtaking feats. While Elizabeth watched safely from the ground, Katherine thrilled the crowds by performing her loop-the-loop and another one of her favorite stunts, the nosedive. The nosedive looked particularly frightening. Katherine would take her plane about 1,500 feet in the air. From this height, she would point the airplane straight down and dive a thousand feet. At the last possible instant, at about 100 feet above the ground, she would pull the plane's nose up and level off, leaving breathless spectators fearing that she would crash.

Katherine Stinson taking off in her Wright biplane at the Barnes County Fair in North Dakota, in July 1914.

Katherine had dinner with Elizabeth after her California performance. The show had been a success, but Katherine was unhappy. "It's not enough to perform the same stunts everyone else does," she moped. "I want to keep doing things no one has ever done before. If I can't stay one step ahead of other pilots, the public will have no reason for wanting to see my air show rather than theirs."

Elizabeth thought she knew part of the reason for Katherine's worries. That morning the paper had printed a comment made by Brigadier General Bliss, Commander of the Southern Department of the Army, remarking on Katherine's flying. Bliss said that Katherine "must not attempt to 'loop-the-loop' in the air or execute other aeronautical stunts that are dangerous to her life." On reading the paper, Katherine had fumed, "Wind currents make me do some stunts that are not premeditated?!" Bliss's statement was ridiculous!

Katherine flashed a look of determination. "I have an idea for a new stunt, one using Chinese fireworks," she declared. Elizabeth cringed as she pictured Katherine plunging to her death, her plane burning brightly in flames set off by the fireworks.

"That's not what I had in mind," Katherine said, noting Elizabeth's discomfort. "I can safely attach a magnesium flare to my plane and use it to write in the sky at night."

Elizabeth knew better than to tell Katherine that she couldn't do this stunt. Whenever anyone told Katherine that a thing couldn't be done, Katherine only worked harder to prove that it could be accomplished. So Elizabeth decided to adopt a wait-and-see attitude.

She did not have long to wait. On December 17, 1915, the night sky over Los Angeles became as bright as day when Katherine traced the initials "C-A-L" for California across a background of stars using a white magnesium flare tied to the wing of her plane. Katherine wrote so precisely, and the night sky was so clear, that photographers were able to take pictures of her feat. Next, she looped, flew upside down, and dropped in a spiral to within 100 feet of the ground, leaving a glorious shower of sparks trailing behind.

Katherine Stinson had become the first person in the world to perform night skywriting.

Chapter 8

Canadian Flying

Katherine spent much of 1916 crisscrossing the North American continent. She began her first Canadian tour in June 1916. Very little flying had yet occurred in Canada; the Canadian military air service was yet to be born. Katherine used her plane to give bombing exhibitions at the Sarcee army camp. The officers, who had never even imagined using planes to drop bombs, were very impressed with the ways airplanes could change strategies for waging war.

One of Katherine's proudest moments came while visiting a Sioux tribe in Brandon, Manitoba. The Stinson children were one-fourth Cherokee by birth. Katherine's flying performance so impressed the tribal elders that, under the sponsorship of Chief Waukessa, Katherine became a princess of the Sioux. She had her picture taken in front of her Partridge-Keller Looper airplane with

In 1916 Katherine Stinson was declared a "Princess of the Sioux" under the sponsorship of Chief Waukessa in Brandon, Manitoba, Canada.

more than forty tribal members wearing full ceremonial regalia, complete with feathered head-dresses.

Katherine certainly had her share of close calls while flying in Canada. She told reporters of one such incident that summer:

> It was one of the most curious experiences I ever had. Before I went up, there was the usual crowd around the machine, examining it and looking into the cockpit where I sit. Just before I started, a woman came up to the machine and said that she had dropped her glove in there. I looked for it and felt around under the seat, but couldn't find it.
>
> When I got into the air I found that I couldn't turn to the right. I tried it over and over, but, no! The pulley was jammed, and I couldn't make anything but a left-hand turn. It made me pretty uncomfortable and I couldn't understand it. I kept fussing away, hoping to get the pulley free, but it simply wouldn't work. By maneuvering around, I managed to land safely. And when I investigated, there was the missing glove, caught in the mechanism of the controls.

Because she had been such a huge success at Camp Sarcee, three weeks later Katherine decided to pay a visit to another Canadian army camp, Camp Hughes, also near Brandon, Manitoba. She neglected to phone or wire ahead to let the army officials know that she was coming. Much to her surprise, when Katherine landed her airplane on a green grassy field just outside the camp, she was promptly arrested. Always one to keep her cool, even under the most difficult circumstances, she calmly explained to the provost marshal that her mission was to entertain, not to spy. "In that case," replied the provost marshal, "please carry on!" More than 60,000 troops came to see Katherine's exhibition.

Flying back to Brandon, Katherine's plane broke a piston, and she was forced to land in a wheat field. The long wheat stalks grabbed the plane's undercarriage and promptly turned it over on its nose. Gasoline began spilling from the fuel tank. Out in what she thought was the middle of nowhere, Katherine was more worried about losing precious gasoline that would be hard to replace than she was about her plane catching on fire. She jumped out of the cockpit and crammed a rag into the gas pipe.

Once the flow of fuel was stopped, Katherine began looking around for the nearest farmhouse where she could get help. Within a few minutes, a farmer in bib overalls and chin whiskers showed up. "Is that one o' them new-fangled threshing machines?" he asked. Katherine burst out laughing. She was continually amazed at the ideas people came up with when they had never before seen a plane. After she explained the plane's workings to the farmer, he helped her push the plane's tail down so that it would be in the proper position for a takeoff. While Katherine went to phone for help, the farmer stood guard over her plane.

Performing stunts for her audiences was one of Katherine's favorite flying feats. She particularly enjoyed doing the nosedive, because it was always an audience thriller. In fact, on her last flight in Canada, at Regina, Saskatchewan, Katherine plunged so steeply during her nosedive that eyewitnesses were sure she crashed. From miles around, people called the town's switchboard to report that they had seen her plane go down. Katherine, the supreme performer, had safely pulled out of the dive at the last moment and headed back to the United States for more flying exhibitions.

Edith Dodd Culver never forgot the first time she met Katherine, at the Virginia State Fair in October 1916. "Katherine Stinson was a surprise to me," recalled Mrs. Culver, the wife of one of the four army pilots who had established the U.S. airmail service. "I suppose I expected her to be mannish. Instead, she was something quite the opposite, fragile and dainty. Her friendliness and soft refined voice masked unbounded endurance and courage. She was a brunette with long chestnut curls fringing her checkered cap. She was definitely feminine. She was America's sweetheart of the airways at that time as surely as Mary Pickford was America's sweetheart of the silent screen."

As night fell on the state fair, the Culvers waited while Katherine revved up her motor and lit the magnesium flares attached to the lower edges of her plane's wings. Shortly, someone with a megaphone announced that the great aviatrix would make a daring night flight above the field. She would execute the difficult figure-eight maneuver. Mrs. Culver remembered it well:

> She took her place in the open cockpit, strapped her safety belt, pushed the visor of her checkered cap around, tucked her curls up into it to keep them out of her eyes. Shorty Shroeder spun the wooden propeller with one swing to start the motor and signaled Katherine away. She opened the throttle, taxied to the end of the racetrack, and the next thing we knew she was in the air! . . . Katherine made her figure-eights as the crowd watched, spellbound.
>
> Afterwards we were to sit around the campfire and talk about flying until the dying embers reminded us that it was time for Shorty to stake the plane down, swathe the engine in canvas, and then for all of us to go to the hotel for a good night's rest.

That night remained in the observers' memories long afterward.

Early pilots like Katherine Stinson had to lean to one side to help turn their planes. Since seat belts were not widely used then, many pilots plunged to their deaths by falling out of their seats while attempting these turns.

Chapter 9

Opening a Flight School

As the year 1916 drew to a close, the United States was buzzing with news of war in Europe. Katherine, back in San Antonio, called a family meeting with her mother, her sister Marjorie, and brothers Jack and Eddie. Katherine was anxious to take part in the war effort. With two pilots in the family, Marjorie and herself, she had figured out a way to participate.

"Listen, everyone," Katherine gathered their attention. "San Antonio is a perfect place to open a flight school and train pilots for the war. The weather is grand for flying nearly all year long. I've found about five hundred flat acres just outside town that can be used for the airfield. I think I can get it for a good price." Katherine's eyes gleamed as she spoke of her new project.

The four Stinson siblings: Jack and Marjorie in the car, Eddie and Katherine in Katherine's plane.

"The only problem, as I see it, is that I'm scheduled to go to Japan and China in a couple of months to perform. There's no way I can be in two places at once, running a flying school in Texas and flying in the Orient at the same time. That's where you come in. Will you run the school in my absence?" she asked her family. Eighteen-year-old Marjorie was instantly sold on Katherine's idea. She loved to teach as much as she loved to fly. A flight school would be just the thing to satisfy both desires.

Katherine's mother, Emma, ever the practical one, also loved the idea. She thought the school would be a natural extension of the Stinson Aircraft Company, and she wasted no time drawing up plans for the Stinson School of Flying.

On January 18, 1916, the Stinson family asked the San Antonio City Commissioners to grant them a lease on 500 acres of land. During that meeting, Marjorie testified that "the rich and leisured class regard flying as a sport and recreation, and will furnish many pupils to the aviation school. The only objection I have to this land," she said, "is that a small part of it has recently been set aside by the city for a cemetery. For amateur aviators high in the air to look earthward and see graves being dug as if for their reception is not conducive to good flying."

The next day, the city commissioners approved the lease, and the Stinson School of Flying was officially in business. The school's flying field became one of the first three private airports in the United States. Eddie, Katherine's younger brother, was assigned the task of clearing the mesquite trees from the property. Marjorie, who already had one student, a San Antonio banker named Jack Frost, knew that many other young Texans were eager to learn the new art of flying.

Katherine used money she had made from her exhibition flying shows to finance the new school.

Marjorie, who already had been dubbed "The Flying Schoolmarm," and Katherine were the school's faculty. Their mother took care of administrative duties (and raised a few chickens on the side). A couple of mechanics, Dan Kiser and Richard Hand, rounded out the school's staff. One month later, the Stinson School officially opened.

Marjorie was a no-nonsense woman when it came to teaching. She later described her training methods in a magazine article:

> Being a woman, I felt that I had a right to talk a little, and so plunged into an explanation of why the plane flew and how. I explained that in flying they had only three things to consider: namely, the direction (left or right), the banking, and the ascent or descent.
>
> Since aviation was itself new, I felt that I could perhaps make myself clearer by citing examples with which they were all familiar. An auto, I told them, had only one way in which it could be controlled: namely, direction. In a plane this corresponded to the rudder. Next, I mentioned a motorcycle, and the fact that it could be both banked and guided, and that likewise a plane could be both banked and guided by using the ailerons and rudder respectively. Finally, the airplane came up for discussion, with its added maneuverability due to the function of the elevator.
>
> The boys listened patiently and politely. I concluded the lecture with a promise to permit each man to assume as much control of the plane as he could safely handle. And I promised to ground anyone who did not release all control at a given signal from me and allow me to land the plane in case of trouble. The air is no place to settle a difference of opinion about how to fly, as they were all obviously stronger than I was. I pointed out a fire extinguisher within my reach on the plane, and explained its double duty.
>
> The first flights, or joy hops, were of about ten minutes' duration each, and were to get the

embryo pilots used to being up and to give them a chance just to look around. Afterward came short flights on which I allowed them to handle the rudder control. We had tied a white string on the skid brace out in front as a check on straight flying and properly executed turns. Overcontrol or undercontrol with the rudder resulted in the string flying back at an angle, and the error was corrected by flying in the direction in which the string was pointing. The string would also serve as a stall indicator, but I did not tell them about that and how to correct it, because if they stalled to where the string registered, it was just too late anyhow.

After about twenty minutes' practice on the rudder, they were given both the rudder and ailerons to handle. Flying then began to be a little

Marjorie Stinson, known as "The Flying Schoolmarm," trained over eighty pilots for World War I. She taught them at the Stinson School of Flying in San Antonio.

intricate, as they were flying eights, or making left and right turns alternately, and around given points, in serious preparation for their solo license test. We made wide, easy turns at first, gradually tilting the plane and tightening the turns until they could make a sixty-degree bank with confidence. Here they began to develop flying instinct.

After classes they would discuss their various discoveries or faults, and these discussions were most helpful. Soon they were sufficiently advanced with the rudder and ailerons, and were given the elevator, thereby doing all the flying. I merely sat in the plane and folded my hands. On many occasions I had to unfold them pretty quickly and get the plane out of a tight place.

As soon as errors could be corrected without my help, I gave my pupils an added worry—the prospect of an emergency landing. I took each man up separately, stopped the engine, and had him make a landing without power. Such a landing would be part of their license test, so just how it was done was a subject for consideration. Spot landings without power were an every-flight occurrence.

The first flying class graduated late in November 1916. All five new pilots qualified for their FAI certificates on December 29 of that year. Eddie Stinson qualified for his license that day, too. Eddie had worked as a mechanic, or "grease monkey," on his sisters' planes and had always wanted to be a pilot. Katherine and Marjorie consistently refused to teach him to fly because he was known to drink alcohol excessively, and they feared for his safety.

Nevertheless, Eddie had practiced and practiced on the school's Wright airplanes and qualified for his flight certificate. Even though his sisters wouldn't teach him, Eddie had taken a few lessons the previous September while in Dayton. These lessons, combined with his practice flights in San Antonio, gave him the flying experience he needed to pass his flight test and earn flying license certificate number 375.

Katherine and Marjorie taught together for a month before Katherine had to leave for the Far

East. Katherine was to travel to Japan by ship, with two of her dismantled airplanes carefully crated in marked boxes and safely stored in the ship's hold. Early in her flying career, Katherine had become a good mechanic. She understood engines and knew how to take her entire plane apart and put it back together again. When traveling to air shows, she often traveled by train and carried her plane on the train as cargo. She disassembled the plane for the trip and reassembled the plane at her destination. As a result, she was quickly able to spot potential mechanical problems before they occurred.

"The important thing is to be as careful as you possibly can to have every part of your engine and of your plane in perfect condition," Katherine said. She always put her plane in perfect order before attempting her breathtaking stunts.

Katherine departed for the Far East with her friend Elizabeth and her mechanic, Frank Champion. The trip across the Pacific Ocean to Japan took nearly a month. Katherine often entertained Elizabeth late into the night with tales of what it felt like to fly:

Flying is not like anything else in the world. The problems are different, and so are the sensations. Even when you are going a hundred miles an hour you do not seem to be moving; it is the earth that is rushing along below you. When you leave the ground, it does not seem as if you are going up, but as if the earth were sinking away from you. It is as if in motoring you came to a down-hill, and instead of staying on the ground, you simply went on into space.

As you go higher everything on the ground flattens out. The hills sink until they look like little mounds. A big building dwindles until it is like a pool of thread standing on a table. If you are over rough water, big waves look like mere ripples. And, by the way, you can see straight down into water, so that the bed of it is perfectly clear to you, even at a depth of fifty feet or more. That is why airplanes are so valuable in hunting U-boats. Submarines can hide from ships, but an aviator can look down into the water and see them; while of course the men of the submarine are blind so far as seeing the plane is concerned.

When you go up, at first the people below you are plainly visible. You can tell boys from men; you can see the women, dogs, horses, and so on. At a thousand feet, boys and men look alike. At two thousand feet, you can't tell any of these apart. Finally they become mere moving specks.

People have shown so much curiosity about tailspins that you may like to know what the sensations are in doing one. Suppose I am flying at our field near San Antonio and go into a tailspin when I am over two thousand or more feet up. It isn't safe to start one below that, because, if you did, you would not have altitude enough to come out of it.

When I start the spin, the plane goes round and round with the motor as its axis. My seat is several feet back of the motor, so that, as the plane whirls on the motor, as on a pivot, I am going around in circles back of it. The impression is of an earth gone mad; houses chasing lakes around in an ever-widening circle. For as you come down nearer to the ground, the landscape spreads out around you.

Finally, I reverse my rudder, push forward the controls, and am flying along easily and naturally. Looking behind me I see San Antonio to the left and the lake several miles to the right, calmly where they belong, just as if they had not been chasing each other in great rings around my plane.

The air is not one even medium, like water is below the surface. It has its own hills and valleys, made by air currents. It has holes, or pockets, into which you drop unexpectedly. It has bumps and irregularities. Flying in a strong and gusty wind keeps you busy every minute.

Katherine loved the brisk salty sea air, but she grew restless during the long ocean voyage. She could hardly wait to reach Japan, unpack her planes, and once again fly through her beloved skies.

Katherine Stinson wearing a few of the numerous flight medals she won during her illustrious career.

Chapter 10

Soaring the Skies of Japan and China

Katherine began setting records the minute her plane hit the Japanese sky. She was the first woman to fly in the Orient.

Japanese women in particular were thrilled by Katherine's show and viewed Katherine as their emancipator. In Japanese society, women played a subservient role to men, and Katherine's flying was seen as a triumph for womankind. She dared to do things that only men were allowed to do at that time.

Katherine also set the imaginations of Japanese youth on fire with her aerial performances. Katherine Stinson fan clubs sprang up all over Japanese cities. The fan mail response was overwhelming. In one letter, M. Yoshimura, a Tokyo schoolboy, struggled to express in English his feelings on seeing Katherine's debut performance:

> Welcome! How waiting we were that you come. I read your skillful arts and looping in the newspapers. And last night when I saw you that you were flying high up in the darkest sky I could

not help to cry: you are indeed Air Queen! This word is not fair speech. Madam, I wish you health and happiness for purpose of airoplain society for long, long time. Madam, please remember that I am a Japanese student and wanting to make myself air-man if I can.

These moving words portray the feelings of many people whose lives Katherine touched with her flying exhibitions.

In Japan, larger crowds than those she drew in the United States turned out to see her. Nearly 25,000 people came to her Tokyo performance on December 15, 1916. When she drew an "S" in the night sky using Chinese fireworks, the spectators cheered nonstop for ten minutes. When Katherine finally landed her small airplane, she was nearly crushed as the Japanese crowd gathered to get a close-up view of this female flier.

That night she told Elizabeth, "I came closer to dying on the ground today than I ever have up in the air. Mother was right to be worried about my safety on the ground."

"I think I have a solution to the problem," Elizabeth said. "Why not arrange for your landing strip to be well away from the crowds, perhaps with an auto waiting nearby to whisk you away?" she proposed.

"What a perfectly splendid idea!" Katherine exclaimed, jumping up from her chair and twirling her friend around the room. "That way, I can avoid the crowds and reporters until I've had a chance to catch my breath and can greet them properly." Katherine had already added a mirror to her plane so she could wipe the grease from her face and apply make-up before meeting the public.

Katherine was often exhausted at the end of a flight. Not having a windshield on her airplane, it took Katherine tremendous effort just to keep her head erect against the eighty-mile-per-hour winds. By the time a flight was over, her neck was so tired that it often took all her will power just to hold up her head. The idea of a brief rest after a flight appealed to Katherine greatly.

At the next show, a car was waiting away from the crowd to meet Katherine on landing. Word soon got around of this scheme, and when she landed near her car a week later, Katherine found it heaped with flowers and floral arrangements presented by officials.

Katherine's love affair with the Japanese continued. She made her third flight dressed in Japanese costume, priceless embroidery given to her by a prominent Japanese social leader.

Katherine's tour of Japan proved a blazing success. Her daring feats inspired crowds wherever she flew. And her courage helped many to attain their own personal dreams and goals.

The next journey for Katherine and Elizabeth was to China, where Katherine flew thirty-two exhibition flights. On Sunday, March 11, 1917, her first show in Peking was commissioned as a private performance. The exhibition was held on the sacred grounds of the Temple of Agriculture. Leading Peking citizens, including the foreign minister, watched Katherine's premiere performance.

Thousands more gathered at vantage points outside the temple as Katherine performed three consecutive loop-the-loops, leaving a trail of smoke blazing behind her plane to mark her accomplishment. Her Chinese audience watched with open-mouthed amazement, as they had never seen anyone fly through the air in a machine, much less perform the aerobatics maneuvers Katherine flew so effortlessly. At the end of her performance, Li Yung Hung, China's president, presented Katherine with a magnificent diamond pin.

Peasants and noblemen alike gathered to watch the young American woman perform her daredevil stunts. While making a nose-dive during one of her performances, the rudder control snapped off in her hand. All that remained of the control, which guided the plane's direction, was a small piece near her feet.

Katherine was forced to fly "blind" for short stretches because she could not see over the plane's dashboard when she bent down to reach the remains of the rudder control on the floor. She had to bob up and down in the cockpit to get her bearings, first making small steering corrections, then monitoring her position in the air. Her great skill enabled her to land the plane safely.

Asked what some of her next goals were, Katherine told a correspondent for *China Illustrated Weekly* in March 1917 that she planned to "attempt a nonstop coast-to-coast flight upon her return to the U.S." Her ambition was to break the current nonstop distance record set in November 1916 by Ruth Law, her chief competitor. "The plane I plan to use is already under construction as we speak," she told the reporter.

Katherine Stinson in her modified Wright biplane. Note the lack of windshield and her name emblazoned on the plane. This airplane was little more than a glorified kite with wheels, wings, a tail, and an engine.

Katherine was so competitive that she had nearly canceled her trip to the Orient. She badly wanted to challenge and beat the record that Law had set. Instead, Katherine decided to travel to the Orient after all, for two reasons: her exhibition arrangements and dates had all been set, and the plane she intended to use to break the record wasn't yet ready.

Before she left China, President Li Yung Hung again presented gifts to Katherine—a silver loving cup and a personal check for several thousand dollars. The cup, awarded to "Miss Shih Lien Sun, Granddaughter of Heaven," bore the inscription, "A Thousand Li in the Twinkling of an Eye." The cup remained one of Katherine's most cherished possessions throughout her life.

Katherine and her party returned to Japan in April 1917. The Japanese Island Empire enchanted Katherine, and her popularity remained unsurpassed. Everywhere she went, Katherine was treated and entertained like royalty. The Japanese showered her with valuable gifts at every turn.

Katherine's suitcases overflowed with cloisonné vases, loving cups, silver and gold medals, and other mementos of exquisite workmanship. A Tokyo firm of pearl divers gave her a beautiful necklace of pearls arranged as miniature airplane propellers.

Although Katherine loved Japan and the Japanese people, she reluctantly cut her second trip short because the United States had entered World War I. In April President Wilson had asked Congress for a declaration of war, giving the U.S. permission to officially enter the war and send troops overseas to fight. On May 6, 1917, Katherine, Elizabeth, and Frank embarked for the United States, where Katherine eagerly expected to join the U.S. war efforts as a pilot. Within three weeks, Katherine and her entourage were back on the U.S. mainland in San Francisco, California.

Stinson Field: A San Antonio Legacy

Stinson Field in San Antonio, Texas, was created in 1916 as a result of the vision of Katherine Stinson and her family. Today it is the second-oldest continuously running civilian airport in the United States.

When the Stinsons established the airport and flight school in San Antonio, they focused international attention on the city, contributing to its development as a center of aviation.

After training eighty-three pilots for World War I, the Stinson School of Flying was closed by government order once the war got underway, and the city took over the airfield. In 1928 Texas Air Transport (later American Airlines) began commercial flights at Stinson Field, joined by Braniff Airlines in 1935 and Eastern Airlines in 1938.

In 1936 the city officially named the airport "Stinson Municipal Airport," in honor of its founders. The terminal building, erected by the Works Progress Administration, still serves as the main terminal today.

In the early 1940s, the new San Antonio International Airport was built, and the U.S. Army Air Corps began training World War II pilots at Stinson Municipal. After the war, the commercial airlines moved to the new airport, and Stinson Municipal became a "reliever" airport for the new facility.

Stinson Field is located south of downtown San Antonio, approximately fifteen minutes from the central business district, at 8535 Mission Road. The field features the Texas Air Museum, which houses historic aircraft. An actual engine used by Katherine Stinson in 1914 is on display on a replica of a Bleriot plane. Stinson Air Center is also located at the airport. It is a school that teaches airplane and helicopter flying and aerobatics.

The spirit of the Stinsons shall always be a part of Stinson Field. The last wishes of both Marjorie and Jack Stinson were that their ashes be scattered over the field.

Katherine in front of the JN-4 plane she used in her Red Cross "bombing" mission.

Chapter 11

Red Cross "Bombing" Mission

After her return to the United States, the Red Cross soon approached Katherine to ask for her help in raising money for wounded soldiers. Katherine quickly agreed to make a fundraising tour from Buffalo, New York, to Washington, D.C. Katherine's mission was to "bomb" several cities along her route with Red Cross leaflets and then land her plane and collect pledges for money. Katherine made this entire flight on her own initiative and at her own expense, as a contribution to the war effort.

Katherine arrived in Buffalo two days before her scheduled "bombing" flight in order to purchase a new airplane, a Curtiss machine. Unfortunately, the company had a backlog of orders and couldn't deliver her plane for an entire month. Undeterred, Katherine secured permission to use a government plane instead. Before beginning her actual flight, she spent fifteen minutes training in the air in a brand new government JN-4 plane. The "Jenny," as the plane was nicknamed, was larger than any plane Katherine had flown before and had a ninety-horsepower engine.

A drizzling rain greeted Katherine as well-wishers gathered to see her takeoff on Sunday, June 24, 1917. As she left Buffalo, New York, low black clouds covered the sky. She followed the New York Central railroad tracks to her first stop in Rochester, New York. By early afternoon the sky cleared, and Katherine made good time, buzzing over Little Falls, New York, and dropping Red Cross pledge leaflets. The townspeople, who had been waiting all afternoon to be "bombed" by Katherine, were thrilled.

Approaching Albany, New York, Katherine leaned over the side of her plane and saw the Empire State Express train headed for the city. Always a great competitor, Katherine waved at the passengers and raced the train. She won, beating the train into Albany by thirty-four minutes.

After collecting pledges in Albany, she stopped in New York City, Philadelphia, and Baltimore. Katherine, well known for using any old map she could get her hands on, had a map showing the route from Buffalo to Albany, but not from Albany to New York City. Once in the air, she simply followed the New York Central Railway tracks. When asked why she didn't follow the Hudson River, she replied, "Because I'm afraid of the water." For the remainder of the flight, she used an ordinary railroad map she picked up in the train station, found in a folder published by the Pennsylvania Railroad.

Katherine was waylaid for two and a half hours in Philadelphia while people scrambled to find enough gasoline for her to finish her tour. Finally reaching Washington, D.C., she circled the Washington Monument once before landing.

Katherine's 670-mile journey had taken a little over eleven hours of flight time, and she had raised $2 million in pledges for the Red Cross—an average of nearly $3,000 a mile.

In Washington, D.C., a huge crowd awaited her, cheering her pluck and skill. On the steps of the U.S. Treasury building, she delivered to Secretary of the Treasury William G. McAdoo the checks for the fund, letters, and credentials that she had gathered during her journey. Accepting these from Katherine on behalf of the Red Cross, McAdoo said, "I congratulate you upon your wonderful achievement. You have shown that you possess the same spirit that is characteristic of the true Red Cross worker. You dare to face danger and even the possibility of death itself in the performance of your duty. You have done your duty and done it well."

Later, when asked about flying through wind and inclement weather, Katherine said:

> While your engine is going, you do not hear the wind. But if you shut off your motor, the wind, cut by the wires of your plane, fairly shrieks. For a long time I didn't have a windscreen on my machine, and the thing that tired me most in flying was the way the wind blew my head back. The force of it, constantly pressing against my face, was terrific. It always made the back of my neck ache with the effort to hold my head steady against it. Even with a shield in front, the air rushes in at the sides, and often I duck my head down quite inside the body of the machine to get away from the wind.
>
> When you fly in the rain without a windshield in front, it is like being peppered with buck-

Katherine Stinson presenting Secretary of the Treasury McAdoo with a check for $50,000, collected during he $2 million "bombing" mission.

shot. The raindrops sting your face like sleet driven by a gale. I have been flying when a thunderstorm would come and the lightning would streak right between the wings of my machine. It is a very curious thing to see it so close to you. I wasn't in the least frightened at the time. But later, when I heard of an airplane being struck by lightning when it was up in a thunderstorm, I decided not to take any more chances of that kind.

When you are flying toward a cloud it does not seem as if you, yourself, are moving. The cloud seems to be rushing at you. And when you enter it you are in the thickest fog you ever imagined. You can't see the wings of your plane. I have been in clouds so dense that I couldn't even see my own hands operating the controls. You immediately lose your sense of direction, and, especially, you can't tell whether you are going up, or down, or on an even keel.

Katherine was acutely aware of the dangers of aviation. "Engine trouble and carelessness are the two great dangers of flying," she wrote:

You can guard against the latter, and to a certain extent against the former. But in spite of the fact that the motors we have are a hundred percent better than when I began flying six years ago, you never can be absolutely sure of them. And if you do have engine trouble, one thing is certain: you are going to come down, one way or another. How you do it is a matter of life or death to you.

You never know at what minute this constant menace may become a present danger. So you are always looking down, watching the panorama below you, with one thought in the back of your mind: Where can I land if I have to do it now?

The summer of 1917 was drawing to a close. Not satisfied with simply raising money for World War I, Katherine was determined to enlist in the armed services. She applied to the U.S.

Army's aviation section, but an application from a woman was so unusual that she was forced to wait months for an answer. The army's reluctance to enlist Katherine was ironic, since they weren't hesitant to use her ideas. World War I combat flyers were being trained to execute stunts, including many of the aerobatics maneuvers she had invented. Initially, Katherine had been criticized for performing these stunts. Now the army wouldn't give her the opportunity to use these flying techniques to help win the war.

72

Marjorie, Emma, and Katherine Stinson.

Chapter 12

Running the Stinson Flying School

While Katherine was busy flying exhibitions and raising money for the war effort, the Stinson Flying School was meeting its own challenges. In January 1916 the school had fourteen pupils and four working aircraft. By the end of March 1916, twenty-four fledgling pilots were studying, and the school's future began to look very bright as the demand for pilots increased. Rumors circulated of government grants becoming available to pay for training reserve pilots. An increasing interest in South Texas aviation seemed certain.

Meanwhile, friction was growing between Mrs. Stinson and her son, Eddie. After obtaining his pilot's license, Eddie, a "nat-

*Stinson School of Flying around 1917, which later became Stinson Field.
A Wright Model "B" airplane can be seen in the hangar doorway. Today, Stinson Field in
San Antonio is the second-oldest continuously running civilian airport in the U.S.*

ural-born" aviator, wanted to spend as much time as he could in the air. His mother tried her best to keep him on the ground. Mrs. Stinson constantly criticized Eddie for his drinking, wanting to keep him in the mechanic's shop, where he could be watched. Ruling the school with an iron hand, Mrs. Stinson forbade idle gossip. She hated it when people whispered behind her back. Eddie's personality was completely opposite his mother's; he was known for being good-natured and completely irresponsible. The two fought constantly with each other, each determined to have his or her own way.

One of the major problems the Stinson School faced was plane crack-ups, which were often daily occurrences. Because flying was such a new endeavor, the planes themselves were still in the experimental stages, with non-standardized parts and equipment. Often a plane would be put together by scavenging parts from three or four other planes. The planes broke apart easily, especially in the hands of the inexperienced pilots. But the only way anyone knew to teach flying at that time was to take the new pilots up in an airplane and give them a "go" at the controls.

During the summer exhibition season of 1916, Katherine, Marjorie, and Eddie headed up to Chicago, and at Ashburn Field they assembled new airplanes. Katherine and Marjorie each had identical planes built by Brock, a pilot of international reputation, with the assistance of Eddie. These Brock "loopers," as they were called, were assembled and flying by midsummer. Katherine left almost right away to tour the Northwest, while Marjorie began instructing a new class of Canadian students. Although Marjorie made a few exhibition flights in her Brock, she soon cracked it up in a landing mishap.

Despite this misfortune, Marjorie, like Katherine, wasn't afraid to fly. "I feel perfectly safe," Marjorie said, "as long as I am high above the ground. Safety lies in elevation. One does not have to contend with chug-holes and air-puffs, and the trees and telephone poles are out of the way. Of course, if one goes up very high and remains there too long a terrible chill comes on; the fingers become numb and there is danger of not being able to control the machine. I have been out of sight of the earth several times. At an altitude of 10,000 feet, the carburetor of my engine becomes thickly covered with frost and I am chilled through and through!"

Meanwhile, Eddie made a name for himself as an aviator by flying Katherine's Brock. At the same time, Eddie took on a pupil, Robert F. Shank, who had tried to teach himself flying. Shank had bought a two-seater plane but was unable to figure out how to get his plane airborne. One attempt to lift off almost killed him. After that, Shank installed dual controls in his plane and enlisted Eddie's aid to teach him to fly. When the summer exhibition season was over and the Stinsons returned to San Antonio, Shank joined them as an instructor and mechanic for the flying school.

Eddie Stinson is credited with developing a new flight technique for recovering from a tailspin. Prior to this discovery, hundreds of pilots had been killed when their planes dropped into this deadly maneuver. No one knows whether Eddie made his discovery by accident or on purpose.

A tailspin occurs when the plane is not only headed straight down toward the ground, but is also rolling or spinning as it heads down. The tendency is to pull back on the elevators, causing the airplane to climb, but that reaction just increases the spin. The plane's stick controls two different sets of equipment: the elevators and the ailerons. The elevators are located on the back side of the plane's horizontal tail and make the plane go up or down. When the stick is pulled back, toward the pilot, the airplane climbs. When the stick is pushed forward, away from the pilot, the airplane dives. Moving the stick from side to side engages the ailerons, which are located on the back of the plane's wings. The ailerons cause the plane to bank or roll.

During a tailspin, the pilot's first reaction is to pull back on the stick, forcing the airplane to climb. However, this mistaken impulse caused hundreds of pilots to crash to their deaths. Eddie found that shoving the stick forward and forcing the plane to dive, rather than pulling the stick back toward the pilot to try to force the plane up, stopped the plane's spin.

Mrs. Stinson purchased three engineless Burgess biplanes for $350, plus an eighty-horse-power Curtiss OX engine. Using the best parts from each of the three planes, Eddie and Bob Shank managed to put together one airworthy machine using the OX engine. This Burgess plane became the school's advanced trainer, and Shank was in charge of training pilots on it. Neither Eddie nor his sisters ever flew the big biplane. Mrs. Stinson also hired Gilbert "Bud" Budwig, a civilian instructor with the army, to work part-time with the Burgess biplane.

One cloudy morning, Budwig took a trainee up for a test ride so that he could check out the trainee's flying skills. While trying to climb through the overcast sky, the new pilot put the Burgess into a spin. Bud grabbed the wheel and tried to pull the plane back level, but there was nothing he could do—the plane's controls were locked up. The plane crashed into the mesquite bushes and trees. The fliers were lucky to be taken to the hospital, rather than to the undertaker. The Burgess wasn't as lucky.

However, there were apparently enough leftover parts to rebuild the Burgess, because the Stinsons still had two trainers flying on August 1, 1917. Unfortunately, the Wright trainer lasted only a week more before S. Benton Davies stalled it near the ground on his first solo flight. The machine was completely destroyed and turned into kindling. The second plane, the refurbished Burgess, was also doomed. Its novice pilot overshot a landing and slammed into Mrs. Stinson's chicken coop. When the chicken feathers finally hit the ground, there was nothing flightworthy left at the school. Then the government banned all civilians from flying. The school was prevented from giving any more lessons, and its assets were soon sold. By the time the Stinson School of Flying closed, Marjorie had trained eighty-three pilots for World War I.

Chapter 13

Setting New Records

Katherine, always on the lookout for new records to make and break, chose a nonstop flight from San Diego, California, to San Francisco as her next challenge. One of Katherine's dreams had been to break the U.S. distance record. Katherine's arch flying rival, Ruth Law, had set a new record in November 1916, flying nonstop from Chicago to New York, a distance of 590 miles.

Katherine had a reputation for flying by whatever map she could find, whether a page torn from a geography book or a map picked up at a railroad station. This flight, however, would cover over 600 miles. She had her map

Katherine Stinson in her Curtiss airplane. The design of the plane has changed dramatically—it has an enclosed cockpit and windshield.

carefully mounted on rollers so that she could turn the map as the landscape passed beneath her plane.

Here is how Katherine recounted her bold undertaking:

I awoke before dawn on Tuesday, December 11, 1917. The sky was overcast and the weather chilly. I had to catch a ferry from San Diego to North Island where my Curtiss plane was waiting. The ferry hadn't arrived, so I decided to have some breakfast. Just as the waitress brought my meal, I heard the toot of the ferry's loading whistle. I gulped down half a boiled egg, grabbed a piece of toast and ran to catch the ferry. We were halfway across the bay before I remembered I hadn't paid for my meal.

Once on North Island, I gave my plane a final check and took off for San Francisco at 7:31 A.M. An Army plane escorted me as far as Oceanside, then rocked its wings in a salute and headed back to San Diego. Now I was truly on my own.

Two hours later, I passed through the heavy fog banked over Los Angeles and headed due north. I was using the tracks of the Santa Fe Railroad as my guide. I approached the Tehachapi Mountains and encountered strong winds, which caused my plane to buck and rock all over the place. I began to rise gradually over Tehachapi Pass. I eased the plane up to 9,000 feet, the highest I'd ever flown in my life.

I knew that aviators had tried to cross it and failed and I knew, too, that once over the top I would have no trouble the rest of the way. As I passed the summit, the highest point of the mountains, I breathed a sigh of relief, for I thought the most dangerous part of my flight was behind me.

I looked down to check my position with the railroad tracks and nearly panicked. The tracks were nowhere in sight! Not knowing what I had done wrong, I decided to continue flying due north using my compass as my guide. A few minutes later, which felt like hours I assure you, I spotted the railroad tracks again. Apparently, the tracks had vanished into a tunnel the train used to get through that part of the mountains. I had never been so happy to see railroad tracks in my whole life!

I flew over Bakersfield around noon. By this time I was famished and feeling faint from hunger. Looking down, I saw people going home for lunch and imagined I could smell the food cooking. I was so tempted to land and get a bite to eat. I couldn't of course, I would ruin the non-stop flight if I did. Besides, I was determined to be the first person to travel from San Diego to San Francisco between meals!

Often I could see big caterpillar tractors plowing below, and my thoughts went way back to the women working in the fields of Japan. Towns, cities, farms, hills, and mountains passed rapidly. The cold head wind blew into my plane; it cut my lips and chilled me, but I never had any fear. The main thing was speed.

I had packed my knitting with me, thinking I might get in a few stitches, but I found myself having to concentrate on staying on course. The knitting might have taken my mind off food, but I couldn't afford to stray off course because I had just enough fuel for the 610 mile flight with hardly a pint to spare.

As it happened, I landed in San Francisco at 4:41 P.M. with only two gallons of gasoline left in the gas tank. With that amount of petrol I could have driven twenty or thirty miles in an auto, but it was barely enough to get a hiccup out of my plane. Luck was with me once again on this trip.

And the reception I received when I landed! As I circled the San Francisco harbor, boats of all kinds shrieked, hooted, whistled, and tooted in the loudest welcome I've ever received. Tears came to my eyes as I heard the cheers of thousands of soldiers down below. They were lined up in two files at the Presidio, an army fort in San Francisco, and I landed between them. They rushed up and helped me out of my plane and I was mighty proud. It's one thing to read a passage in a book, "and the crowds roared," but I tell you, my ears rang for three days afterward from the cheering of that crowd.

I set a new national record that day for both distance and duration, covering 610 miles in nine hours and ten minutes. I'll bet Ruth Law is glad a girl and not a man broke her record. Believe me, I was tired that night. Just try sitting in a chair for nine hours without moving and you'll know what I mean.

Now that she had finally broken Ruth Law's record, Katherine had only her own record to beat.

Katherine Stinson making her way through the crowds in Presidio, California, after setting a national record for distance and duration—610 miles in nine hours, ten minutes.

Chapter 14

From Chicago to the Big Apple

In March 1918 Katherine finally heard from the army about her application to be a World War I pilot. Although she was known as perhaps the greatest female aviatrix in the world, the army turned down her request to fly for them. Despite the fact that she could outfly almost any male pilot she challenged, the army felt that war was no place for a woman and refused to commission her as a pilot.

Heartbroken, she went to Chicago, where she set a new duration record of ten hours and ten minutes' flying time. She did this by flying from Chicago to New York.

Remembering how hungry she had been during her record-setting California flight, Katherine was determined not to repeat that mistake on this day in June 1918.

Katherine Stinson competing against a race car around the track at Cicero Field in Chicago. She loved to race cars in her plane and always won. "Stinson" is painted on the plane's wings, and the magnesium flares are lit.

I learned a lesson from that California experience, and when I started for New York from Chicago, I had a friend put up a lunch for me. My machine had the old style of steering gear: a lever for each hand instead of the single rod used by most pilots now. This makes it a good deal of a problem to use your hands for anything else. I told my friend to put my lunch in a paper bag, and I tied this to one of the uprights. Then I had hot coffee in a thermos bottle, which I wired to another fixture; for of course everything has to be fastened in so that it won't fall out if you do any stunts.

Eating luncheon that day was a hectic performance. I was going over Fremont, Ohio, and the inhabitants must have thought I was a very eccentric flyer or was giving them a special exhibition. I would let go of one lever long enough to get the bag down or the thermos bottle unfastened; for my friend, in mistaken care, had wrapped each one separately in paraffin paper. Then the machine would side-slip, or do something else, and I would have to drop everything and right it.

I had been sick in bed for five days before I made that flight. The evening before I started, the weather man in Chicago, who had been watching conditions for me, called me up to say that the next day would be fair, with a 15-mile wind from the east. Of course that would be a head wind and unfavorable for me. If the normal speed of a machine is, say, 100 miles an hour, it can only make 85 miles against a 15-mile wind. Whereas it could make 115 miles if there was a following wind. But the weather man said this was the best he could promise as far ahead as he could prophesy.

I went back to bed and thought things over. I was pretty weak and shaky and had a high temperature, but I had set my heart on making that flight. After all, you have to choose which is going to rule, your mind or your body. I believe it is a matter anybody can decide. If you determine that it shall be your mind, your body will surprise you by the way in which it bucks up and behaves itself.

After I had thought the thing over, I dressed, called a taxi, and went to the hangar. With the mechanic, I went over my machine carefully, gave him all the directions about extra gasoline and so on, and went back to bed. At four-thirty the next morning, I went to the hangar again, gave the machine another minute examination, and at six-thirty I was off. If the wind had been favorable, I should have made the flight to New York without stop. As it was, I broke both the distance and endurance record in this country. That seems to me more worthwhile than staying in bed with nothing to show for it but doctors' bills.

Having proven herself as a distance flier, Katherine decided to concentrate on the challenge of carrying airmail.

Katherine Stinson checking out the skies before a flight.

Chapter 15

Carrying Airmail Across North America

Katherine continued her treks crisscrossing the North American continent. She wound her way to western Canada in late June 1918, winging her Curtiss airplane over wide prairie stretches and visiting the ranching communities tucked away in the countryside. Katherine arrived in Calgary on July 9, 1918, when the Calgary Exhibition was in full swing. The exhibition showed the remarkable harvests of this area, which was called "The Great Grain Basket of the Dominion."

Promptly at 6:00 P.M. that evening, Katherine opened the throttle of her plane and bumped over the gopher holes of a field north of the city. In a second, she was airborne, seeking an altitude of 5,000 feet. Two hours and five minutes later, she swooped to a graceful landing in Edmonton. In her cockpit, Katherine carried a pouch containing 259 letters, which she personally hand delivered to the postmaster of Edmonton when she landed. With this flight, Katherine became the first civilian to fly the airmail in Canada.

Katherine Stinson doing what she loved best, getting ready to fly. Although this plane has an enclosed cockpit, note that there's no windshield.

There wasn't enough room for both the mail and Katherine's suitcase in the plane's cockpit, so Katherine sent her suitcase to Edmonton from Calgary on the fast express. The train left Calgary at 3:00 P.M., three hours before Katherine's plane took off on the same journey. Her suitcase arrived in Edmonton at 9:30 P.M. The suitcase had taken six and a half hours to make the journey, while Katherine's plane took only two hours. She had to wait until her suitcase arrived to change out of her grease-stained clothes!

Inspired by her success in flying airmail in Canada, Katherine next decided to fly airmail for the United States Postal Office. Soon she was knocking on the door of Ben Lipsner, the aerial mail superintendent. "Women," she told Mr. Lipsner, "should have some place in the new airmail flying corps, and I'm the best woman flier around."

Lipsner was somewhat taken aback by this gutsy young woman. He didn't quite know how to handle Katherine, so he listened carefully and courteously. "I'll take the matter under advisement," he told her. "Please leave me your application and I'll consider it sometime in the future," Lipsner said, stalling for time.

Proud of how he handled the situation, Lipsner didn't expect to hear from Katherine again. Little did he realize just how determined this "Flying Schoolgirl" was to obtain an airmail job. Leaving Lipsner's office, Katherine headed straight to the postmaster general's office, where she convinced Alfred Burleson that she was uniquely qualified for the position.

Burleson, the postmaster general, remembered Katherine from her mail-delivering days in Montana and was completely won over by Katherine's feisty charm. He issued a directive to Lipsner: "Add Katherine to the five-man airmail pilot group." Lipsner remained unconvinced of Katherine's abilities, but he knew better than to openly question his boss's decision. Cunningly, he thought he knew a way to get around having Katherine be an airmail pilot.

During their initial interview, Katherine had told Lipsner that the only planes she could fly were the ones equipped with the old Wright two-stick control mechanism. All of Lipsner's mail planes were outfitted with the new one-stick system with rudder bar controls. Lipsner told Katherine she couldn't fly the mail unless she could handle the new equipment. Undeterred, Katherine asked that a mail plane be specially outfitted for her. Lipsner said flatly, "Impossible!" As Katherine stormed out of his office, Lipsner was sure that he had won that round and would never hear from Katherine again.

Katherine wasted no time in marching straight over to Burleson's office. Burleson soon issued a second directive to Lipsner: "The little lady is to be given any type of equipment she wants, regardless of cost."

Lipsner knew when he was beaten. He ordered a special two-stick mail plane prepared for Katherine. On September 26, 1918, Katherine's first flight as an official employee of the Post Office Department took place. There was only one airmail route at the time: Washington–Philadelphia–New York. On her initial flight, she flew with pilot Maurice Newton as her escort. The pilots each carried about 150 pounds of mail as their planes took off from Washington. Newton's plane led Katherine's all the way to New York as planned and landed first at Belmont Park.

The next day it was Katherine's turn to lead the two planes on the airmail flight back to Washington from Philadelphia. For unknown reasons, newspaper reporters announced this second flight as a race, which of course it wasn't. When Katherine landed first as planned, the press proclaimed Katherine the "winner." Understandably, Newton was furious, as were other members of the Aerial Mail Service. Without stating any reason and with no fanfare, Katherine resigned from the airmail service almost immediately. She never told anyone why she resigned.

Both Katherine and her flying competitor Ruth Law repeatedly attempted to enlist in the army, but they were refused because they were women. Ruth was so furious about her rejection that she wrote in an article for the magazine *Air Travel*, "It would seem that a woman's success in any particular line would prove her fitness for that work, without regard to theories to the contrary."

Ruth was later asked by both the army and the navy to fly officially as a recruiter for the armed services, which she did. While traveling in that capacity, Law was allowed to wear the uniform of a noncommissioned officer, the first woman in U.S. history to officially do so.

Still disappointed by the army's refusal to let her participate in the war, Katherine wrote her mother: "It seems to me there is always somebody to tell you you can't accomplish a thing, and to discourage you from even attempting it. If you are going to let other people decide what you are able to do, I don't think you will ever do much of anything."

Two weeks after her mother received this letter, a telegram from Katherine arrived at the Stinson household.

DEAR MOTHER STOP GOING TO FRANCE STOP
WILL DRIVE AMBULANCE FOR THE RED CROSS STOP
SEE YOU AFTER THE WAR STOP
LOVE KATHERINE END

In France, Katherine drove ambulances for Mrs. Harriman's Ambulance Corps with the same determination and courage she had shown flying her planes. She worked fearlessly night and day to transport wounded soldiers from the battlefield to the hospital. Neither bombs nor bullets scared the woman who had braved night flying, long-distance flying, and daredevil stunts.

Katherine worked endlessly, with such energy that she literally drove herself to exhaustion. On November 11, 1918, the war ended. The Allies had won, but Katherine was just beginning a new battle.

Katherine Stinson with one of the ambulances she drove in France during World War I for Mrs. Harriman's Ambulance Corps.

Katherine Stinson wearing her trademark blue checkered cap.

Chapter 16

From Aviation to Architecture

At the end of World War I Katherine returned to the United States. The damp weather in France and the tireless hours she spent driving an ambulance had ruined her health. While driving Red Cross ambulances, she contracted influenza, which later developed into a more serious disease, tuberculosis. The illness forced her complete retirement from aviation in 1920.

Katherine's illness brought her near death, and she entered a sanitarium in New York in an attempt to regain her health. Katherine finally moved to Santa Fe, New Mexico, where she entered the Sunmount Sanitarium to continue her battle against tuberculosis, which was a major killer at the time. While in Sunmount, she met John Gaw Meem, a renowned architect. He and Katherine became fast friends. Katherine, always an avid student, soon developed a keen interest in architecture.

Although she had no formal training in the field, Katherine quickly learned architecture, with the help of Meem's mentoring and through her own determination and interest. For seven years, she fought and finally won her battle with tuberculosis. Katherine beat the disease through a treatment of rest and withdrawal from her previously active life.

Her health restored, Katherine married Miguel A. Otero Jr., a veteran airman and prominent attorney who later became a district court judge. The war had taken its toll on her health, and she was never again to fly a plane through her beloved skies.

Instead, Katherine began a new career as an architect. She designed several fine homes in Santa Fe, including the lovely adobe home she and Miguel lived in for the rest of their lives. She also built and remodeled twelve other homes in Plaza Chamisal, the compound where their home was located.

During Katherine's second career as an architect, she remodeled old buildings and designed new ones in the Pueblo Revival Style that was being popularized by her good friend Meem. She opened her own office in downtown Santa Fe. Katherine soon gained recognition for her outstanding work and won many awards in statewide design competitions. Meem would later include her among Santa Fe's important architectural influences of the 1920s and 1930s.

Years after Katherine had given up flying, reporters continued to seek her out and ask questions about her career.

As I said before, I have never had a serious accident. Once I came near it when I was doing the stunt of "writing" something in the air with the smoke from a smudge pot on my machine. For some reason, the smudge pot "back-fired" and one of the wings caught fire. I came down right away without any difficulty. After I landed, I burned my hand a little putting out the fire, and that was the only thing that happened to me. But it was reported all over that I had been almost killed.

People often asked me if I ever "ran into" birds in the air. If I ever have, I didn't know it. My brother once caught an owl on his plane and brought it down with him, but I think that is a very unusual experience.

Once, when I had engine trouble and had to land in a little field, my machine didn't stop before it ran into some trees at the farther end. I climbed out and trudged off to a farmhouse to telephone to the nearest town for assistance. The telephone wouldn't work, so I tried several other houses. But nobody's phone would work, so I went back to the machine, where I found a gang of disgusted telephone men and discovered that my plane had struck the wires and carried them all down. I hadn't been conscious of it.

Did she miss flying? Maybe. But over the years, flying had changed a great deal. "In the early days," she explained, "it was fun to fly. You could soar over rooftops and trees, or drop down to meet a passing train and wave at the engineer. The whole sky belonged to you. Now there are so many regulations. The sky is crowded. All the fun is gone."

Katherine became ill in 1959 and was completely bedridden by 1962. She died on July 8, 1977, at home. She was eighty-six years old.

Katherine Stinson never gave in to fear. She also defied the idea that women lacked the mental toughness to become pilots:

I have found that women are not only just as much interested as men are in flying, but apparently have less fear than the men have. At least, more women than men asked to go up with me. And when I took them up, they seemed to enjoy it.

Apparently fear is not a question of size, or of sex either. One of the pluckiest persons I ever knew was a Chinese woman, the sister of the Minister of War. About six months before I went to China, she had gone up with an aviator, and the machine crashed and she was terribly injured. She was just out of the hospital when I came. And yet the little woman would have gone up with me then if I would have taken her.

Fear isn't a question of size, anyway. If, when I was a little girl, my mother had always been telling me not to do this, and not to do that, not to run, "for fear" I might stumble, not to climb the gate post, "for fear" I might fall, always putting into my mind the idea of being afraid of something, I don't see how I could have had any self-reliance at all. Mother never reproved my sister and me for "playing with the boys." I suppose she thought it would do our little bodies just as much good to be exercised and trained out of doors as it would theirs.

Katherine also saw that fear could be overcome through learning. "Fear, as I understand it," she said, "is simply due to lack of confidence or lack of knowledge—which is the same thing. You are afraid of what you don't understand. You are afraid to attempt something you believe you cannot do."

Katherine Stinson believed in herself, in her abilities, and in her dreams. Although her career as a pilot lasted only seven years, she was a pioneer who helped shape the art of flying as we know it. She will always be remembered as one of the greatest pilots who ever graced the skies.

Glossary

aerodrome:
an early name for an airport.

aileron:
a hinged flap on the rear edge of an airplane's wing, used mainly for lateral control.

Allies:
the nations that united against the Central European powers in World War I or against the Axis powers in World War II. In World War I, these nations included Great Britain, Russia, Italy, Australia, France, the U.S., and many others.

ascension:
the act of rising, as in an airplane or hot air balloon.

aviatrix:
a woman pilot of an airplane.

bank:
the act of turning an aircraft so that one side travels higher than the other side.

biplane:
a type of airplane with two sets of wings; one set above the other set.

barnstorming:
the act of touring rural districts, giving exhibitions of stunt flying, or short airplane excursions.

cloisonné:
a type of jewelry design in which fine wire or thin metal partitions are used to separate colors.

elevator:
an aircraft control, located in the tail assembly, which regulates climb and descent.

emancipator:
a person who frees others, often from some type of slavery.

even keel:
on a ship or airplane, to be level with the water or ground, leaning neither right nor left.

Fédération Aéonautique Internationale (**FAI**):
the first international organization to regulate and license aviators.

horizontal:
parallel to the horizon.

horsepower:
a unit of power applied to an engine, equivalent to 5,500 foot-pounds per second, about 750 watts.

li:
a Chinese word meaning "field" and "earth."

megaphone:
a cone-shaped device used to intensify or magnify the voice.

muslin:
a woven cotton material ranging from lightweight to coarse and heavy, often used to make the wings of early airplanes.

piston:
an engine part that converts the energy from the burning fuel into motion. The piston's motion turns the crankshaft; the crankshaft turns the propeller.

rudder:
a flat piece of wood or metal hinged vertically on the plane's tail, used to control the direction of the aircraft.

subservient:
of lesser rank or importance.

tuberculosis:
an infectious lung disease which, if left untreated, can lead to death.

vertical:
a direction from top to bottom; perpendicular to the horizon.

visionary:
a person with great insight and imagination, expecially when foretelling the future.

Works Progress Administration:
national agency established in 1939 to provide unemployment relief during the Great Depression.

World War I:
the first global war of the twentieth century, lasting from 1914–1918. The U.S. joined the war on the Allies' side on April 6, 1917.

Selected Bibliography

Boughner, Fred. "Series of Disasters hit Stinson Flying School." *Linn's Stamp News,* 10 January 1977, p. 56.

Boughner, Fred. "The Stinsons: Flying sisters end career." *Linn's Stamp News,* 17 January 1977, p. 55.

Brooks-Pazmany, Kathleen. *United States Women in Aviation, 1919–1929.* Smithsonian Studies in Air and Space, no. 5. Washington, D.C.: Smithsonian Institution Press, 1983.

The Katherine Stinson Files. The Women's Collection, Texas Woman's University Library, Denton, Texas: Texas Woman's University.

Keffeler, Christine A. "Katherine Stinson." In *New Handbook of Texas,* vol. 6, p. 105. Austin, Texas: Texas State Historical Association, 1996.

Lomax, Judy. *Women of the Air.* London: John Murray, 1986.

May, Charles Paul. *Women in Aeronautics.* New York: Thomas Nelson & Sons, 1962.

McCullough, Joan. *First of All: Significant "Firsts" by American Women.* New York: Holt, Rinehart & Winston, 1980.

Nolan, William F. "The High-flying Schoolgirl." *Sports Illustrated* (October 18, 1965).

Oakes, Claudia M. "Katherine Stinson." In *United States Women in Aviation through World War I.* Washington, D.C.: Smithsonian Institution Press, 1973.

"An Outline of American History." Department of Humanities Computing, Rijksuniversitet Gronigan, 1999. http://odur.let.rug.nl

Rogers, Mary Beth, Sherry A. Smith, and Janelle D. Scott. *We Can Fly: Stories of Katherine Stinson and Other Gutsy Texas Women*. Austin, Texas: Ellen C. Temple and Texas Foundation for Women's Resources, 1983.

Stinson, Katherine. "Why I am Not Afraid to Fly." *The American Magazine*. (Denton, Texas: Texas Woman's University Library).

Stinson, Marjorie. "Aerial Mail Service in Canada." *The Curtiss FlyLeaf,* vol. 3, no. 1 (July 1918).

Stinson, Marjorie. "The Diary of a Country Girl at Flying School." *Aero Digest,* vol. xii, no. 2 (February 1928): 168–169, 297–298.

Stinson, Marjorie. "Wings for War Birds: How a Girl Taught Fighters to Fly." *Liberty* (December 28, 1929): 25–27.

"Texas Women, A Celebration of History" [touring exhibition], produced by The Foundation for Woman's Resources, Austin, Texas, 1981, on permanent display at the Mary Evelyn Huey-Blagg Libary, Texas Woman's University, Denton, Texas.

Underwood, John. *The Stinsons*. Glendale, California: Heritage Press, 1976.

"Youngest Flyer in America a San Antonio Girl." *Aerial Age Weekly* (April 17, 1916).

Suggested Reading and Internet Sites

Adams, Jean, and Margaret Kimball. *Heroines of the Sky*. Garden City, New York: Doubleday, 1942.

Brooks-Pazmany, Kathleen. *United States Women in Aviation: 1919–1929*. Smithsonian Studies in Air and Space, no. 5. Washington, D.C.: Smithsonian Institution Press, 1983.

Lomax, Judy. *Women of the Air*. London: John Murray, 1986.

Rogers, Mary Beth, Sherry A. Smith, and Janelle D. Scott. *We Can Fly: Stories of Katherine Stinson and Other Gutsy Texas Women*. Austin, Texas: Ellen C. Temple and Texas Foundation for Women's Resources, 1983.

Underwood, John. *The Stinsons*. Glendale, California: Heritage Press, 1976.

Amelia Earhart, American aviatrix, speech entitled, "On the future of women in flying."
Hear this famous aviatrix speak in person about women's role in aviation.
http://www.historychannel.com/speeches/index.html

The Complete Stinson Aircraft Model Directory
Contains history and pictures of different models of Stinson aircraft.
http://www3.bc.sympatico.ca/flightlines/

CrossRoads Access, Inc., Corinth History
1916 Newspaper Abstracts, *The Commercial Appeal,* Vol. CIV #94, Saturday, October 2, 1916. Wonderful newspaper account of Katherine Stinson's adventures at the Tri-State Fair in Memphis, Tennessee. http://www.tsixroads.com/corinth/rt071.html

Hangar 9 Aeroworks

Web site for Stinson aircraft enthusiasts, includes a link to the "World Stinson Database," a listing of over 3,000 Stinson aircraft owners. http://www.hangar9aeroworks.com/108main.html

International Stinson Club

Great web site containing information on the operation, restoration, history, and heritage of Stinson aircraft. http://www.aeromar.com/swsc.html

Katherine Stinson Middle School, San Antonio, Texas

Internet links to Katherine Stinson information. http://www.northside.isd.tenet.edu/stinww/Sms_kath.html

Otero-Stinson Family Papers, 1843–1985

Description of the contents of the Otero-Stinson Family Papers Collection. Center for Southwest Research, General Library, University of New Mexico. Go to "O" for Otero-Stinson. http://elibrary.unm.edu/oanm/index_NmU.html

Smithsonian National Air and Space Museum Aeronautics Division

Biography of Katherine Stinson from the Smithsonian Institute in Washington, D.C. http://www.nasm.edu/nasm/aero/women_aviators/katherine_stinson.htm

Stinson Municipal Airport

Visit Stinson Field in San Antonio as it is today! http://www.ci.sat.tx.us/aviation/page12.htm

Westin's Stinson 108 Voyager Aviation Page

Lots of information on all aspects of Stinson aircraft, including photographs of different styles of Stinson airplanes. http://www.somtel.com/~westin/ac-0.htm

Photo Credits

Pg. iii—Center for Southwest Research, General Library, University of New Mexico, Stinson-Otero Collection, Neg. No. 000-506-0053.

Pg. 8—Center for Southwest Research, General Library, University of New Mexico, Stinson-Otero Collection, Neg. No. 000-506-0720.

Pg. 13—Center for Southwest Research, General Library, University of New Mexico, Stinson-Otero Collection, Neg. No. 000-506-0135.

Pg. 17—Center for Southwest Research, General Library, University of New Mexico, Stinson-Otero Collection, Neg. No. 000-506-0130.

Pg. 20—Center for Southwest Research, General Library, University of New Mexico, Stinson-Otero Collection, Neg. No. 000-506-0056.

Pg. 22—Center for Southwest Research, General Library, University of New Mexico, Stinson-Otero Collection, Neg. No. 000-506-0104.

Pg. 26—Buehman, Center for Southwest Research, General Library, University of New Mexico, Stinson-Otero Collection, Neg. No. 000-506-0503.

Pg. 30—Center for Southwest Research, General Library, University of New Mexico, Stinson-Otero Collection, Neg. No. 000-506-0151.

Pg. 35—K.C. Anderson, Center for Southwest Research, General Library, University of New Mexico, Stinson-Otero Collection, Neg. No. 000-506-0125.

Pg. 38—Center for Southwest Research, General Library, University of New Mexico, Stinson-Otero Collection, Neg. No. 000-506-0072.

Pg. 40—McFarland Photo, Center for Southwest Research, General Library, University of New Mexico, Stinson-Otero Collection, Neg. No. 000-506-0220.

Pg. 45—Center for Southwest Research, General Library, University of New Mexico, Stinson-Otero Collection, Neg. No. 000-506-0505.

Pg. 49—Center for Southwest Research, General Library, University of New Mexico, Stinson-Otero Collection, Neg. No. 000-506-0121.

Pg. 50—Wiles, Center for Southwest Research, General Library, University of New Mexico, Stinson-Otero Collection, Neg. No. 000-506-0127.

Pg. 54—Center for Southwest Research, General Library, University of New Mexico, Stinson-Otero Collection, Neg. No. 000-506-1033.

Pg. 58—Center for Southwest Research, General Library, University of New Mexico, Stinson-Otero Collection, Neg. No. 000-506-0027.

Pg. 62—Center for Southwest Research, General Library, University of New Mexico, Stinson-Otero Collection, Neg. No. 000-506-0116.

Pg. 66—Center for Southwest Research, General Library, University of New Mexico, Stinson-Otero Collection, Neg. No. 000-506-0078.

Pg. 70—Center for Southwest Research, General Library, University of New Mexico, Stinson-Otero Collection, Neg. No. 000-506-0242.

Pg. 73—Aultman Collection, Southwest Collection, El Paso Public Library, #A-3207.

Pg. 75—The San Antonio Express News Collection, The UT Institute of Texan Cultures at San Antonio, No. 85-28

Pg. 80—Center for Southwest Research, General Library, University of New Mexico, Stinson-Otero Collection, Neg. No. 000-506-0086

Pg. 85—Center for Southwest Research, General Library, University of New Mexico, Stinson-Otero Collection, Neg. No. 000-506-0245

Pg. 87—Center for Southwest Research, General Library, University of New Mexico, Stinson-Otero Collection, Neg. No. 000-506-0208

Pg. 89—Center for Southwest Research, General Library, University of New Mexico, Stinson-Otero Collection, Neg. No. 000-506-0047

Pg. 90—Center for Southwest Research, General Library, University of New Mexico, Stinson-Otero Collection, Neg. No. 000-506-0052

Pg. 92—Center for Southwest Research, General Library, University of New Mexico, Stinson-Otero Collection, Neg. No. 000-506-0057

Pg. 96—Center for Southwest Research, General Library, University of New Mexico, Stinson-Otero Collection, Neg. No. 000-506-0084

Pg. 98—The UT Institute of Texan Cultures at San Antonio, #0851-G

Pg. 103—Center for Southwest Research, General Library, University of New Mexico, Stinson-Otero Collection, Neg. No. 000-506-0096

About the Author

Debra L. Winegarten, writer and sociologist, lives in Austin, Texas. She received her bachelor of science degree in sociology with honors from Texas Woman's University and her master's degree, also in sociology, from The Ohio State University. She is a pioneer in research and writing about implementing new technologies in education, paradigm shifts, and online curriculum development. She is the co-author of *Strong Family Ties: The Tiny Hawkins Story*, available from Sociosights Press, P.O. Box 1662, Austin, Texas, 78767-1662. She works as a consultant with those writing their memoirs and family histories.

Winegarten enjoys taking long walks, watching beautiful sunsets, swimming, flute playing, dancing, salsa music, massage, and her cats, Mystic and Chanukah. She loves getting e-mail from her readers! Her e-mail address is: sociosight@aol.com.